THE DISCOURSE ON

# THE ROOT OF EXISTENCE

THE DISCOURSE ON

# THE ROOT OF EXISTENCE

*The Mūlapariyāya Sutta and its Commentaries*

Translated from the Pali

by

BHIKKHU BODHI

BUDDHIST PUBLICATION SOCIETY
Kandy Sri Lanka

Buddhist Publication Society
P.O. Box 61
54, Sangharaja Mawatha
Kandy, Sri Lanka.

Website: http://www.bps.lk

First published 1980
Second edition 2006



National Library of Sri Lanka - Cataloguing in Publication Data

The Discourse on the Root of Existence:
The Mūlapariyāya Sutta and its Commentaries / comp. by Bhikkhu Bodhi, Kandy, Buddhist Publication Society, 2006-108p.; 22 c.m.
ISBN 955-24-0064-3
i. 294.3823 DDC　　ii. Title
iii. Bodhi Himi comp.
1. Tripitaka　　2. Sutrapitaka

ISBN 955-24-0064-3

Cover design & Typeset at BPS

Printed by
Ajith Printers
Boralesgamuwa — Sri Lanka

## CONTENTS

## TRANSLATOR'S PREFACE

Correct understanding of a subject can only arise when the disposition to misunderstand has first been safely set at bay. As long as the disposition to misunderstand persists undetected and uncontrolled, novel ideas even of genius can do little to alter the outlook of those to whom they are addressed. Their inner core of inspired vision will be passed over unseen and their verbal formulations either brushed aside as unworthy of notice or assimilated in terms of the preconceptions they were intended to dispel. On this account they will fail to accomplish their designated purpose—to illuminate or "shed light"—but like flames without fuel, will only exhaust their energy, swallowed up by darkness in the end.

This principle—that openness and unconstrictedness of mind must be secured as the prerequisite for understanding—holds with special force when the subject to be communicated is the Dhamma, the teaching of the Buddha, which cuts across the grain of our habitual patterns of thought. Before the new and radical ideas of the Dhamma can sink into the mind and execute their function—to enlighten and to liberate—the subjective propensities obstructing their proper apprehension must first be put away. Only when the inclination to wrong understanding has been effectively removed can the receptivity essential to right understanding be ensured. Only when the mind has been made "fit, pliant, unhindered, uplifted, and serene" can the liberating, doctrine be absorbed.

Out of regard for this principle, the two major collections of the Buddha's discourses contained in the Pāli Canon—the Dīgha Nikāya or "long collection" and the Majjhima Nikāya or "middle length collection"—each open with a sutta designed to clear away the obstructions preventing a right grasp of the teachings to follow in their trail. These obstructions take the form of subjective misconceptions—errors of outlook and attitude which may be either adhered to at the theoretical level in the form of views, doctrines, and beliefs, or clung to emotionally as the expression of forces more deeply ingrained in the makeup of the psyche. In either case the misconception will act as a filter to remove from the message information the subject does not wish to hear, or as a refractor to distort the message to bring it into conformity with his own predilections.

The Brahmajāla Sutta, the first discourse of the Dīgha Nikāya, aims at eliminating the hindrance of erroneous views; it does this by elaborating a "net" of sixty-two cases capable of containing all theoretical stands on the primary issues of speculative thought, the nature of the self and of the world. Though shorter in length than the Brahmajāla, the Mūlapariyāya Sutta, the first discourse of the Majjhima Nikāya, is even larger in scope, for it sets itself the aim of exposing the whole mass of subjective misconceptions, from their branches down to their roots. It deals not only with wrong notions born of speculation, but with those sprung from conceit, craving, and other defilements as well. Brief as it is, this compact discourse reveals the entire structure of man's egocentric orientation towards the world. It points out the chain of conditions that keep man tied in his mundane bonds, and the essential knowledge he must win to break the bonds and realize genuine freedom. As both its title and position imply, the Mūlapariyāya Sutta is the most fundamental of the Buddha's discourses found in the Pāli Canon. It is the concentrated essence of the teaching, packing into its enigmatic statements profound truths of ontological, epistemological, and psychological significance.

The present work is a parallel to my earlier treatment of the Brahmajāla Sutta, published under the title *The Discourse on the All Embracing Net of Views.** It offers an English translation of the Mūlapariyāya Sutta, "The Discourse on the Root of Existence," along with its commentarial exegesis, essential for understanding the many difficult passages occurring in the primary text. The exegetical material consists of a commentary and a subcommentary. The former is included in the *Papañcasūdanī*, the complete commentary or *aṭṭhakathā* to the Majjhima Nikāya, composed by Bhadantācariya Buddhaghosa in the fifth century C.E. on the basis of the ancient commentaries he edited. The subcommentary or *ṭīkā*

* Buddhist Publication Society, Kandy, 1978.

has the dual purpose of elucidating key terms occurring in the commentary and of explicating knotty points left over from the sutta. It is regarded as the work of Bhadantācariya Dhammapāla of Badaratittha, who is sometimes assigned to the sixth century.

In my own presentation I give the sutta first in its entirety without the commentary. This is followed by the exegetical section, containing the commentary almost in its completeness (omitting remarks of exclusively grammatical and etymological interest), with selected passages from the subcommentary, particularly those bearing on the philosophical and psychological significance of the discourse. There are fewer selections from the subcommentary in the present work than in my treatment of the Brahmajāla Sutta, as the Mūlapariyāya subcommentary confines itself more to annotation than to independent investigation, the distinguishing feature of the Brahmajāla subcommentary. The passages selected from the exegetical works have been arranged in an interwoven pattern to accord with the unfolding of the sutta. Phrases in parenthesis are my own additions, inserted for the sake of clarity.

The present translation was undertaken and completed at the request of the Venerable Nyanaponika Mahāthera, who read through the typescript and made a number of useful suggestions. For his constant advice and encouragement I am grateful. I am also grateful to my teacher, the Venerable Balangoda Ānandamaitreya Mahā Nāyaka Thera, who encouraged me in my first attempts at a rough translation of the Mūlapariyāya commentary. Lastly, I must express my appreciation of the late Mr. R.G. de S. Wettimuny. It was a series of discussions with the late Mr. Wettimuny in 1973 that opened my eyes to the depth of the Mūlapariyāya Sutta, and eventually stimulated my own attempt to understand and interpret the discourse. For any errors of translation or exposition I myself take full responsibility.

Bhikkhu Bodhi
October 1977

## List of Abbreviations

All editions Pali Text Society (PTS), unless otherwise noted.

| | |
|---|---|
| AN/A | Aṅguttara Nikāya |
| Cy. | *Majjhima Nikāya Aṭṭhakathā* (Commentary) |
| DN/D | Dīgha Nikāya |
| Dhs | Dhammasaṅgaṇī |
| It | Itivuttaka |
| J | Jātaka story |
| Ja | *Jātaka Aṭṭhakathā* |
| MN/M | Majjhima Nikāya |
| Nidd I | Mahāniddesa |
| Nidd II | Cullaniddesa |
| Paṭis | Paṭisambhidāmagga |
| SN/S | Saṃyutta Nikāya |
| Sn | Suttanipāta |
| Sub. Cy. | *Majjhima Nikāya Ṭīkā* (Subcommentary) |
| SVibh | Suttavibhaṅga: Pācittiya section |
| Th | Theragāthā |
| Ud | Udāna |
| Vibh | Vibhaṅga |
| Vism | *Visuddhimagga* |

To the right of the slash, references to A, D, M, and S give the volume and page number of the PTS edition of the work referred to; e.g., M I 10 . To the left of the slash, references to DN and MN give the number of the sutta; when followed by a dot and another number, e.g., MN 12.3, the latter number is the paragraph number.

References to AN and It give the "book" or section (*nipāta*) number and the sutta number, e.g., AN 4:3 is the fourth sutta of the "section of fours".

References to SN give the *saṃyutta* ("collection") and sutta number, e.g., SN 1:1 is the first sutta of the first *saṃyutta.* References to Ud give the sutta number.

References to Paṭis give the chapter and paragraph number as given in Bhikkhu Ñāṇamoli's translation of the work: *The Path of Discrimination* (Pāli Text Society, London, 1982).

References to Sn and Th give the verse numbers. References to J give the Jātaka story number.

References to Vism follow the chapter and paragraph number of Bhikkhu Ñāṇamoli's translation of the work called *The Path of Purification,* 3d ed. (Buddhist Publication Society, Kandy, 1975).

References to Dhs give the paragraph number as given in Mrs. C.A.F. Rhys Davids' translation of the work: *Buddhist Psychological Ethics* (PTS, 3d ed., London, 1993).

References to Vibh give the chapter and section of the Pāli text, followed by paragraph number in Ven. U Thiṭṭila's translation of the work, *The Book of Analysis* (Luzac & Co., London, 1969).

## Texts Used

### Primary Sources

1. Majjhima Nikāya: Mūlapaṇṇāsapāli; Burmese-script Chaṭṭhasaṅgāyana (Sixth Great Council) edition; Rangoon, 1956.
2. *Majjhima Nikāya Aṭṭhakathā (Papañcasūdanī): Mūlapaṇṇāsa-Aṭṭhakathā*; Chaṭṭhasaṅgāyana edition; Rangoon, 1957.
3. *Majjhima Nikāya Ṭikā: Mūlapaṇṇāsa Ṭikā* by Bhadantācariya Dhammapāla; Chaṭṭasaṅgāyana edition; Rangoon, 1961.

### Previous Translations Consulted

1. I.B. Horner, trans. *The Collection of the Middle Length Sayings (Majjhima-Nikāya)*, Vol. I; Pali Text Society edition; London: Luzac & Co., 1954.
2. Nāṇamoli Thera, "*The Mūlapariyāya Sutta*" unpublished manuscript translation. Now published in *The Middle Length Discourses of the Buddha,* trans. by Bhikkhu Bodhi and Bhikkhu Ñāṇamoli; Wisdom Publications, Boston, 1995.

# Introduction

That our spontaneous interpretations of our perceptual experience are often undermined by other perceptions which reveal their falsity is a common occurrence met with countless times in everyday life. We see a snake on the ground, and look again to find it is only a piece of rope. We see a pool of water ahead on the road, and find it disappears when we reach the spot where it lay. We look up at the stars at night, and take them to be scintillating sources of light, yet learn that many of these stars are long extinct, being now only dust motes sucked up in the cosmic void.

Since ancient times thinkers of different ages and cultures have seen in this contradictory character of sense perception a fact of deep philosophical significance. Their reflections on this theme have led to a host of explicative theories, some calling into question the reliability of our cognitive apparatus, others the reality of the external world. Yet despite the doubts and disagreements these thinkers might entertain regarding the veracity of our perceptions, there is one fact which has always seemed so evident and so obtrusive as to be beyond questioning. This is the reality of the perceiver itself. That the subject of perception and knowledge exists, as accessible to introspection as colours are to sight—this is a thesis held to be so indubitable as to qualify for the most basic truth of our experience. It is the pivot of our common sense orientation towards the world and the foundation of philosophical investigation alike. Even Descartes, who was ready to drive his fireside skepticism to the point of dismissing the whole domain of perception as an illusory exhibition conjured up by some cunning demon, was in the end led back by the very fact of his doubting to the inevitable conclusion: "I think, therefore I am." And so it is in all traditional modes of thought, from the most rugged common sense realism to the most abstruse metaphysical idealism. All concur in affirming the reality of the subject behind the process of cognition, the one who senses, thinks, and knows.

Yet, it is just this notion of a self-existent subject that the Buddha takes as the target of his teaching, revealing it to be a mere assumption unverifiable in experience. In any of its guises—whether as the "I" of ordinary thought, the soul of religion, or the ego of philosophy—it remains a cognitive ghost, a conception without counterpart in reality. However, according to his teaching, this notion of separate selfhood is no simple innocuous blunder or careless slip in philosophical reasoning. To the contrary, it is a deleterious error with serious repercussions upon the whole of our emotional and volitional life. The notion of an ego is the anchor of our impulses to grasp and to possess, the root of our attachments and aversions, and via these, the root of our suffering. It brings us frustration and dissatisfaction, sorrow, pain, anxiety, and despair; it draws us on through the cycle of existence, as we build up with each of our ego-affirming acts the immeasurable suffering of the *saṃsāric* round.

The Mūlapariyāya Sutta is a discourse delivered by the Buddha for the purpose of exposing the workings of the ego-conception as it inserts itself into the field of perception, bringing its derivative defilements in its train. The sutta, according to the traditional account, originated in response to a particular incident. As related in the commentary, five hundred bhikkhus who were formerly brahmins, scholars of the Vedas, became swollen with conceit on account of their learning, thereby falling away from their spiritual duties. Recognizing the situation, the Buddha spoke this sutta to shatter their pride and thus render them open to instruction once again. But though originating under specific conditions, the sutta's message transcends the time and circumstances of its genesis, for its theme is nothing less than the core of the Dhamma itself—the problem of suffering and its cessation. In a series of short, cryptic, staccato utterances, the Buddha discloses the way the ego-notion imposes itself on the process of experience, twisting the data to fit its own picture as to how reality should be. He shows how this egocentric bias engenders craving and the cyclic pattern of existence, and how by correcting the illusion of a separative ego, craving may be eliminated and the round of suffering brought to a halt.

The sutta unfolds in four major sections explaining the cognitive pattern of four types of individuals, each in relation to twenty-four possible objects of cognition. The four types of individuals are the "uninstructed worldling" who lacks understanding of the Dhamma and so repeatedly yields to the play of the ego-consciousness; the "learner" who has seen through the falsity of the ego-notion and is working for its full elimination; the arahat or liberated one who has achieved emancipation from the bonds of egoistic clinging; and the "Tathāgata," the Buddha, the originator of the teaching he has discovered through his own unaided realization. These individuals and their cognitive patterns will be treated more fully below.

The twenty-four objects or "bases" *(vatthu)* of cognition cover the entire scale of experiential data, classified in a number of mutually complementary ways. The first set comprises the four primary elements—earth, water, fire and air, symbolic representations for the basic behavioral patterns of matter—extension, cohesion, radiation, and oscillation. The next set of categories takes a tour through the planes of existence recognized by traditional Buddhist cosmology, proceeding upwards from the lower classes of creatures comprised under the collective term "beings" *(bhūta),* through the ascending classes of gods in the sense-sphere heavens and Brahma-worlds, up to the purely mental beings of the four immaterial planes. The next group reclassifies the cognitive objects into four classes of sense-data—the seen, heard, sensed (via smell, taste, and touch), and the mentally cognized. Finally the last group distributes the bases into four abstract categories: the dichotomy of diversity and unity pertaining to sense perception and meditative absorption, respectively; the totality or "allness" apprehended in mystical experience or posited intellectually; and nibbāna, the supreme goal as conceived in the different contemplative systems.

## The Worldling

The first expository section of the sutta gives an account of the cognitive pattern of the "uninstructed worldling" *(assutavā puthujjana),* the ordinary person of mundane concerns who neglects the ariyans, the wise and holy sages, and therefore lacks both the understanding and practical discipline needed to dispel the operations of the ego-consciousness. The worldling's cognitive process, according to the text, passes through a number of stages, each of which reveals a different dimension to his underlying mental constitution. The first phase stated in the sutta is: "He perceives earth as earth" (letting earth serve as a paradigm for any of the twenty-four bases). The "perceiving" referred to here is not, as the text's wording might seem to suggest, a perception which grasps the object in its true nature, as it really is; rather, as the commentary states, it is a "perverted perception" *(viparītasaññā)* already introducing a slight distortion of its datum. We can assume that before this perceiving "earth as earth" supervenes, there occurs a simple, primitive act of perception merely registering the object in a faint and indistinct manner. If the first impression the object makes is lacking in interest, the mind will quickly let it go and pass on to the next. But if the impression is found to merit sustained attention, the object will become the focus of a succession of perceptions bringing its features into sharper relief. These subsequent perceptual acts, however, will not necessarily define the object's nature with exclusively greater clarity and precision. They may grasp more fully the object's prominent qualities; but at the same time, due to the power of ignorance—always present at least dormantly in the worldling's mental make-up—they will also tend to refract the object through subjective distortional media issuing in a false or "perverted" perception. Yet this complex, intricate process occurs so rapidly as to seem to the perceiver a mere automatic registration of the bare perceptual datum. Hence the sutta's wording: "He perceives earth as earth."

Elsewhere in the suttas the Buddha lists four basic kinds of cognitive perversion *(vipallāsa),* each of which may occur at three different levels (AN 4:49/A II 52). The four perversions are holding the foul to be beautiful, the unpleasurable to be pleasurable, the impermanent to be permanent, and the selfless to be a self. The three levels on which these perversions may occur are perception *(saññā)*, thought or cogitation *(citta)*, and views *(diṭṭhi).* The perversion of perception occurs when the object is simply noted through one of the four distortional frames without further development. If the object is subsequently reflected upon in the same mode, there takes place a perversion of thought. And if, through repeated reflection, the conviction arises that this frame yields an accurate picture of the object, the distortion has evolved into a perversion of views.

From the Buddhist perspective these perversions are not inherent products of cognition, but adventitious overlays to the bare cognitive act making their appearance through distinct causes. The factors responsible for the perversions are the defilements *(kilesa)*, headed by lust, hatred, and delusion. The defilements are the cause not only of emotional disturbance, but of cognitive error as well. From their latent condition at the base of the mental continuum, they infiltrate the higher levels of awareness to bring about a fundamental warp throughout the entire body of cognition. This distortion can range all the way from our elementary responses to the data of sensation, through our more complex judgments and beliefs, up to the most sophisticated systems of metaphysical and religious thought. Each provides the founding stratum for the other, the whole structure remaining intact so long as the defilements persist.

The most basic of the three perversions is the perversion of perception, and it is to this that the Buddha alludes in his statement that the worldling "perceives earth as earth." The defilements make their initial impact on the perceptual act by occasioning a wrong mode of attention *(ayoniso manasikāra)* to the objective field, the expanse of sense data which provides the range for perception. The objective field exhibits a variety of features, some of which are potentially provocative of the defilements. When the dormant defilements, through their cumulative force, push for the opportunity to come into the open, they direct the attentional function of consciousness to rivet upon these qualities and revert to them again and again. This "unwise attention" is followed by a series of perceptions which take these qualities as a springboard for imputation. In the act of perception one ascribes to the object certain properties it does not really possess but only appears to possess through the attributive power of the unwholesome mental dispositions. Thus under the influence of latent lust the object will appear beautiful *(subha)* and pleasurable *(sukha)*; under the influence of hatred it will appear repulsive *(paṭigha)*; and under the influence of delusion it will appear permanent *(nicca)* and substantial *(attā)*.[1]. This false imputation, it should be noted, may occur even at the preverbal level of awareness, where the object has not yet been interpreted and rendered conceptually explicit.

The perverted perceptions that result from the latent defilements can in turn spark the defilements to rise up to the surface in an activated form. The perception of an object as beautiful and pleasurable will stimulate lust and the effort to acquire and enjoy it; the perception of something as repulsive will stimulate hate and the effort to destroy it; and the perception of things as permanent and self will harden into dogma and thence bring more delusion. Thus in the working of the worldly consciousness a reciprocal operation comes into view: on the one hand the latent defilements issue in distorted perceptions; on the other, these distorted perceptions awaken the defilements and reinforce their underlying roots. But this whole process takes place with such swiftness and subtlety that the worldling is not aware of it. He does not realize that it is his own mind that has all along been re-modelling the raw materials of cognition to accord with its own propensities, but takes his perceptions to be faithful replicas of things as they really are. Thereby he is deceived, and not recognizing the deception, he goes on to erect upon his distorted perceptions the tower of judgments, values, and convictions that constitutes his mental habitation.

## Conceiving

After perceiving "earth as earth" in the next phase of cognition the worldling goes on to "conceive" his object. This he may do in one or another of four ways given in the sutta: "He conceives earth; he conceives in earth; he conceives from earth; he conceives 'earth is mine.' "[2] Before we can deal with these four modes in their specific implications, it is first necessary to examine the general phenomenon of conceiving itself. The Pali word we have rendered "conceiving," *maññanā,* comes from the root *man,* "to think." But what is indicated by this word is not simple discursive thinking.

This latter is covered by the neutral term *vitakka,* which may be either of a morally wholesome or unwholesome character and may involve either a right or a wrong grasp of its object. The word *maññanā* signifies a different, more developed type of thinking, one that is decidedly unwholesome and always involves a wrong grasp of the object. *Maññanā* is distortional thinking—thinking which, under the domination of defiled predilection, imputes to its object properties or relational implications grounded not in the thing itself, but in the constructive activity of the subjective imagination. It is the tendency of thought to misconstrue its object, building upon the preceding perceptual perversion to apprehend the object in a mode contrary to its actual nature. I have attempted to capture this nuance of the Pali term by translating it as "conceiving," though this English word hardly does justice to the full meaning of the original.

The cognitive distortion effected in *maññanā* consists essentially in the intrusion of the egocentric perspective into the domain of perceptual experience. Experience, from the Buddhist standpoint, is a complex relational field involving the interplay of a multiplicity of factors—evanescent pulses of actuality occurring in functional interdependence without the directive control of an abiding agent. Though fused together in their immediacy into the unity of the cognitive act, these factors can nevertheless be reflectively divided into two reciprocally supportive poles: on the one side, into the cognizing or subjective pole comprising consciousness together with its concomitants; on the other, into the cognized or objective pole comprising the data of cognition. Intermediate between the two stands the sensate organism whose sense faculties provide the necessary meeting-ground for consciousness and its objective spheres. Under the influence of ignorance *(avijjā),* the basic unawareness of the Four Noble Truths, the dependently arisen, egoless components of the experiential field undergo a simplistic reduction in the worldling's mental horizon, crystallizing into an apparent confrontation between an ego and its world as opposed but viable realities. The cognizing pole of the experiential complex presents itself as a subject distinct from the cognitive act itself, the persisting experiencer of each fleeting occasion of cognition. The objective pole in turn takes on the appearance of a world of solid, stable things spread out before cognition as the sphere of the ego's action and concern. From its inner citadel of subjectivity consciousness looks out upon the world as something it may potentially possess; thus it sets out to control, dominate, and manipulate the world as a means of justifying its own implicit claim to an inwardly suspect mode of being.[3]

The emergence of the notion of a separative subject brings in its train the more complex elaborations of the egocentric standpoint, which evolve as attempts to define and identify the elusive ego-entity. The sequence of development the Buddha indicates thus:

> "I am" *(asmi)*—this is a conceived idea *(maññita)*. "This I am" *(ayam aham asmi)*—this is a conceived idea. "I will be" ... "I will not be" ... "I will be with material form" ... "I will be without material form" ... "I will be percipient ... non-percipient ... neither percipient nor non-percipient"—these are conceived ideas. Conceived ideas are a disease, a boil, a dart. (MN 140.31/ M III 246)

The original signification to emerge out of the cognitive warp, this passage makes clear, is the notion "I am," which arises as both a conceit *(asmimāna)* springing from a false estimation or evaluation of objective fact, and a desire *(asmichanda)* expressing a primordial urge for being. Once the notion "I am" comes into the focus of awareness and is taken up as a theme for reflection, it is found to contain a lurking ambiguity. For while the idea "I" is doubtlessly present as a signification of each experience ("I see," "I hear," "I speak," "I do"), it remains a signification that is devoid of content. Conceptually it appears only in the negative, yet it is a strange negative, for it proposes to be the essential purport of the entire experiential event, its irreplaceable center and support. Thus as soon as the notion "I" comes into view as the ubiquitous intention of the cognitive act, it begins to seek a content for itself, the pure negativity of the ego demanding form and shape in the domain of concrete fact. This demand the worldling attempts to meet by identifying the spectral ego with some component of his psycho-physical existence. The result is the conception "This I am," equating the non-apprehensible "I" with the "this," some portion of the five aggregates that constitute the apprehended content. The conviction "This I am" is called "personality view" *(sakkāyadiṭṭhi),* which can assume any of twenty forms depending on whether the ego is identified directly with the aggregates, or seen instead as their possessor, container, or inner nucleus.[4]

Since he has now given some identity to his supposed ego, the worldling next proceeds to speculate about its future destination. At the first level his speculations veer to one of the two metaphysical extremes—either towards eternalism *(sassatavāda)* when he assumes the self to enjoy eternal existence after death ("I will be"), or towards annihilationism *(ucchedavāda)* when he assumes the self to be extinguished at death ("I will not be"). If he accepts the eternalist theory he must then define the mode in which eternal survival takes place. This he does by way of the five alternative characterizations of the self that follow—as "with material form," etc. Thus, beginning from the original egocentric split, the worldling becomes entangled in a net of speculations about his postulated "self" which not only obstruct him from obtaining a clear insight into the nature of reality, but keep him fettered to the round of becoming. It is significant in this respect that the commentary glosses the word *maññanā* by the word *papañca,* which Bhikkhu Ñāṇananda in a penetrating study has explained as the conceptual proliferation that arises through the ingression of the ego-notion into the process of experience.[5]

The activity of conceiving, the commentary points out, is motivated by three underlying mental factors which impart to it its impetus and specific direction. These three factors are craving *(taṇhā),* conceit *(māna),* and views *(diṭṭhi).* Under the influence of craving the egoistic bias comes to expression in thoughts of longing and desire. Under the influence of conceit it becomes manifest in judgments and comparisons whereby we rank ourselves in relation to others as superior, equal, or inferior. And under the influence of views, i.e., the theoretical bent of thought, the ego-bias issues in dogmas, tenets, and speculations concerning the reality and nature of the personal self and its locus, the world.

These three facets of the ego-consciousness respectively occasion the three conceptual constructs the worldling is prone to stamp upon the constituting factors of his experience, namely, the notions "this is mine" *(etaṃ mama),* "this am I" *(eso' ham asmi),* and "this is my self" *(eso me attā).*[6] The construct "this is mine" is a projection born of craving, for it is craving's function to appropriate things as the property of the self. The construct "this am I" is an elaboration of the fundamental conceit, the conceit "I am" *(asmimāna),* the root of later judgments of comparison. And the construct "this is my self" is a formulation of personality view, arising when the repeated occurrence of the thought "I am" is taken as evidence for an abiding self, subsequently identified with the five aggregates. The same triad of mental factors also lies behind the phrase "latent tendencies to I-making, mine-making, and conceit" *(ahaṅkāramamaṅkāra-mānānusaya)* frequently occurring in the suttas.[7] Here, craving functions as the cause for "mine-making," views and conceit as the cause for "I-making," and conceit alone as the "latent tendency to conceit." It is important to translate the terms of this phrase quite literally, even at the risk of awkwardness, in order to stress the fact that the properties of "I-ness" and "mineness" we attribute to things are not intrinsic to the things themselves, but are mere fabrications created by the mind and outwardly imputed to them beneath the shielding screen of ignorance.

In the sutta, the Buddha expounds four modes through which the worldling conceives each of the twenty-four bases. Taking earth as an example, without any interpretive additions, the modal pattern of his conceiving can be rendered thus: "He conceives earth; he conceives in earth; he conceives from earth; he conceives 'earth is mine.' " These cryptic phrases naturally arouse the question as to their exact import. Bhikkhu Ñāṇananda suggests that the fourfold scheme should be understood as an "illustration of the worldling's commitment to the grammatical structure of language," on the grounds that the first three forms of conceiving apprehend the object via a distinct case in the declension of its designative noun—that is, via the accusative, locative, and ablative, respectively.[8] However, while it is true that the three conceiving modes are expressed in accordance with the flexional pattern of language, it is doubtful whether a purely linguistic interpretation does full justice to the situation's depth.

The primary significance of the modal pattern seems to be ontological rather than grammatical. The grammatical element is there to be sure, but it is present only as a derivative of the implicit ontology, not as the principal determinant. On the interpretation here advanced, each mode of conceiving represents an attempt by the worldling (at the pre-reflective as well as reflective level) to give positive being to the conceptual negativity of the intended ego, by positing a relationship between himself as the subject of cognition and the perceived phenomenon as its object. Experience is always thoroughly relational. Things exist not as isolated units, but as participants in a vast network of relationships which can be broken down only in thought and never in fact. The relations things bear to one another are of diverse kinds. They exhibit the relation of identity when two things are considered as distinct instances of a general type, or when the same thing is considered from different points of view; the relation of inherence, when one thing is contained within another; the relation of cause and effect, when one thing emerges from another as its source; and the relation of contrast, when two things are distinguished by different properties or by spatial separation. At the empirical level all these relationships pertain only to observed phenomena, and to these their legitimate application is restricted. However, on account of basic ignorance, the worldling proceeds to construct (either tacitly or explicitly) on the principle of analogy with these empirical relationships, a relationship between what is actually present in his perceptual experience and what can never be present but only presupposed—namely, his "I" or self. Hence, following the relational pattern of observed phenomena, he will tend either to identify with a particular phenomenon "X," when he conceives "X"; or to consider himself as inhering in the phenomenon, when he conceives "in X"; or to consider himself as distinct from the phenomenon, either by way of simple contrast or by way of generation, when he conceives "from X." Or he may seek to appropriate the phenomenon as an accessory of himself in any of these modes. The fourth instance of conceiving, the thought "X is mine," gives separate recognition to this appropriative character of the ego-consciouness; here the worldling reaches out and claims possession over the object, bringing the acquisitive function of craving to a climax.

The phenomenon of conceiving thus turns out to be a double process of identification and appropriation. Through craving the worldling appropriates things as "mine," through conceit and views he identifies with them as "I" or "my self." If conceiving involved only an imaginative projection, as in fantasy or games of make-believe, it would remain a harmless, perhaps even entertaining, preoccupation. However, because the focus of these imaginary constructs is the notion of an ego, a powerful current of emotional energy comes to be invested in the process. And because the notion of an ego lacks foundation, this emotional investment brings only disappointment as the pay-off. It is constantly betrayed by the hard facts of experience, by the impermanence of all that is taken to be permanent "I" and "mine," and the result, for the uninstructed worldling is, eventual suffering.

> The uninstructed worldling regards material form, feeling, perception, the mental formations, and consciousness as the self; or the self as possessing these, or as containing them, or as contained within them. He is obsessed with the thought: "I am material form, etc.; material form, etc., is mine." His material form, etc., changes and becomes otherwise. On this account there arise in him sorrow, lamentation, pain, grief, and despair. (SN 22:1/S III 3)

To the four alternative modes of conceiving, the Buddha adds one more phrase concluding the cognitive pattern of the worldling: "he delights in earth" *(paṭhaviṃ abhinandati).* The verb "delights," as the commentary points out, indicates the operation of craving, like the phrase of the second noble truth describing craving as "delighting here and there" *(tatratatrābhinandinī).* This addition raises the question why, when craving has already been shown as implicated in conceiving, the Buddha introduces it once again under another heading. The reason seems to be to single out a distinct and important facet to the functioning of craving. Any individual mental factor, in the Buddhist analysis, is capable of exercising a variety of functions depending on the diverse contexts in which it occurs, and to bring these different functions into view a corresponding variety of descriptive terms may be necessary. Craving is responsible not only for the perverted perception of objects as pleasurable and attractive, or for the conceiving of things as "mine" and the impulse to acquire them. It is responsible as well for the mental process by which we delight in objects and try to exploit them for the enjoyment we imagine they can yield.

This last aspect, which is the specific connotation of the word "delight," acquires special prominence from the Buddhist perspective because it is the insatiable yearning for delight that maintains the forward movement of the round of existence. When the mind finds satisfaction *(assāda)* in its objects of cognition, it hankers for a constant repetition of the enjoyment. Once its temporary gratification subsides and desire is kindled once again, the search for more enjoyment is taken up anew. Since craving can never be extinguished merely by submitting to its demands, the termination of the physical life-force at death does not bring an end to the vicious circle, but only the opportunity for craving to renew its quest for enjoyment in a new life-form, the heir to the same continuum of consciousness it previously inhabited: "For beings hindered by ignorance and fettered by craving, a renewal of existence takes place in the future on account of delighting here and there *(tatratatrābhinandanā)*" (MN 44.3/M I 299). Thus by stating that the worldling delights in the object, the Buddha indicates by implication that it is the worldly cognitive process which keeps him in bondage to *saṃsāric* suffering. The Buddha himself will explicitly draw the connection later in the sutta when, in the exposition of dependent origination, he declares "delight is the root of suffering" (§13).

The Buddha next inquires into the reason behind the worldling's deluded thoughts of conceiving and delight. Providing the reason himself, he states: "Because it is not fully understood by him." To "fully understand" any particular phenomenon is to comprehend it by way of the three types of full understanding *(pariññā)* mentioned in the commentary: the full understanding of the known *(ñātapariññā),* the full understanding of scrutinization *(tīraṇapariññā),* and the full understanding of abandoning *(pahānapariññā).*

These three phases of comprehension follow one another in successive stages. In the stage of the full understanding of the known, the gross object is analyzed into its constituent "dhammas," and each dhamma delimited in its distinct characteristic, function, manifestation, and proximate cause. This procedure rectifies the common sense assumption of simple substantial unities, disclosing in their place a world of composite wholes made up of impersonal components brought temporarily together through a concatenation of conditions. In the second stage, the full understanding of scrutinization, the dhammas resulting from the above analysis are investigated in terms of their three general characteristics of impermanence, suffering, and non-self; thereby the tendency to perceive things as permanent, pleasurable, and self is countered, and the way opened up for a clear insight into their real nature. Finally, in the third stage, desire and lust for the objects of cognition are eliminated by the full understanding of abandoning.

Since the lack of these three types of full understanding is the basic cause behind the perverted perceptions, conceivings, and delight, the Buddha implies that the way to eliminate these deluded cognitions, which only increase the *saṃsāric* round and the accumulation of suffering, is to develop wisdom—both the mundane wisdom of insight into the conditioned, egoless nature of phenomena, and the supramundane wisdom of the noble path which realizes the unconditioned element, nibbāna.

## The Twenty-four Bases

The same pattern of exposition, working from the perverted perception through conceiving and delight to the lack of full understanding, is applied to each of the twenty-four bases beginning with earth. To explore the conceivings in relation to all these bases individually would require a more detailed discussion than is possible here. However, a few points arising in the sutta do call for comment. Though my remarks will touch only on those conceivings originating through views, it should always be borne in mind that all three factors—craving, conceit, and views—motivate the conceivings of each base. Explanations of the others can be found in the traditional commentary following the translation of the sutta.

The worldling's conceivings of the four elements—earth, water, fire, and air—can be taken to represent his attempts to locate himself in relation to the material world. Compelled by his ignorance to interpret material phenomena in accordance with the egoistic bias of his consciousness, he will incline to conceive material forms either along with the materialists as identical with his self, or with the spiritualists as its tenement, vehicle, or physical instrument.

The conceivings of the bases from "beings" up to the "base of neither perception nor non-perception" express the worldling's ways of interpreting his relation to other sentient beings. Of particular interest here are his conceivings of Brahmā and Pajāpati, two ancient Indian representations of the creator God (though the commentary equates Pajāpati with Māra). Since the divine being is here apprehended as a distinct person, the worldling will not identify with him directly, but he may imagine himself to be in the Divine ("in him we live and move and have our being") or to proceed from the Divine. The conceivings of the four immaterial planes can be understood, in an extended interpretation, as ontological reifications of the corresponding meditative attainments, taken to disclose a transcendental self which is all-pervading (in the base of infinite space), universally cognizant (in the base of infinite consciousness), indefinable in terms of positive being (in the base of nothingness) and indefinable in either positive or negative terms (in the base of neither perception nor non-perception).

The next set of bases classifying the cognitive data into the seen, heard, sensed and cognized, comes into range of the worldling's conceivings when he imputes to the data the properties of being "mine," "I" and "self." The Buddha's later injunction to the learner to refrain from conceiving these objects may be compared to his famous brief instruction to Bāhiya Dārucīriya—an exhortation so deep that it brought Bāhiya to enlightenment right on the spot: "In the seen there will be only the seen; in the heard there will be only the heard; in the sensed there will be only the sensed; in the cognized there will be only the cognized. That is how you must train yourself, Bāhiya" (Ud 1:10/Ud 9). What is to be eliminated from cognition is precisely the false imputations of subjectivity that distort the incoming data and issue in erroneous judgments and beliefs.

The bases of diversity, unity, and allness become the objects of views involving a high degree of philosophical abstraction. Emphasis upon the differentiating aspect of experience prominent in ordinary sense perception leads to a pluralistic ontology extolling the ultimacy of diversity and multiplicity. Emphasis upon the unifying aspect prominent in the meditative absorptions leads to a monistic ontology stressing the ultimacy of a principle of unity—"the One without a second." The idea of totality, arrived at either through meditative experience or intellectual postulation, leads to a philosophy of the pantheistic or monistic type, depending upon the way the "all" is conceptually entertained. The last two positions can be seen as representing the two sides of mysticism, the transcendental and the immanent: the doctrine of unity maintains the transcendent nature of the self or divine principle, the doctrine of totality its immanence or all-pervasiveness.

The last base, nibbāna, here signifies the worldling's conception of the highest goal or ultimate good. The commentary explains it as the five forms of "nibbāna here and now"—indulgence in sense pleasures and the four jhānas. Perhaps this interpretation is too narrow and the notion of nibbāna should be extended to include the Buddhist conception as well, seen from the viewpoint of the uninstructed worldling. But the essential point remains the same—that in his ignorance the deluded person of the world cannot resist the temptation to incorporate even this item, which for the Buddhist means the extinction of egoism and self-referential motives, into the frame of his ego-biased picture of reality.

## The Learner

In the second expository section of the sutta, the Buddha moves on to discuss the cognitive pattern of the learner *(sekha)*—the superior disciple who has transcended the plane of the worldlings and reached the plane of the ariyans, the noble ones or holy ones. In terms of the character typology of the Dhamma, the learner is one of the first three types of ariyan individuals—the stream-enterer *(sotāpanna),* the once-returner *(sakadāgāmī),* and the non-returner *(anāgāmī).* The fourth and last ariyan individual, the arahat, is called a non-learner *(asekha),* not because he lacks learning, but because he has reached the goal of learning, the attainment of final emancipation.

The stream-enterer is a disciple who has penetrated the Dhamma and eliminated the first three of the ten fetters binding to *saṃsāra*—personality view, doubt, and clinging to rules and rituals. He will take rebirth among gods and humans for a maximum of seven lives, after which he will attain final nibbāna. The once-returner, by further development of the path, has attenuated lust, hatred, and delusion, and will return to this world once more before reaching nibbāna. And the non-returner has eliminated the fetters of sensual desire and aversion, thereby liberating himself from all five lower fetters and ensuring his rebirth in the "pure abodes" *(suddhāvāsā)* of the upper Brahma-world, where he will consummate his spiritual training. All the learners remain subject to the five subtle fetters—desire for fine-material and immaterial existence, conceit, restlessness, and ignorance—and therefore still have work to do in order to reach deliverance. But they are all equipped with spiritual faculties capable of developing the path to the end. They can no longer slide back to the level of the worldling, but apply themselves to the training in the higher virtue, the higher consciousness, and the higher wisdom, by which they can eradicate their remaining obstacles and realize their goal. Because they train in the three branches of higher learning, they are called "learners."

In contrast to the worldling who "perceives earth as earth," etc., the learner is said to "directly know earth as earth," etc. "Direct knowledge" *(abhiññā),* according to the commentary, implies the two lower types of full understanding, at least in part—that is, the comprehension of phenomena through their specific marks and conditions, and their scrutinization through the three characteristics. In the Suttas and the Abhidhamma, the word *abhiññā* or its derivatives is often used to indicate the realization of the Four

Noble Truths. Thus, while the worldling and the learner alike perceive the cognitive object in the initial phase of perception not mentioned but merely implied by the sutta, their ways from this point on branch off in two different directions. Whereas the worldling goes on to perceive the object through a perverted perception, the learner discerns the object in its undistorted actual nature. He understands it as a compound of impermanent, conditioned elements embraced by the noble truth of suffering. He knows that the mental and material forces combining in the process of perception originate through prior craving, and that by the eradication of craving here and now through the development of the noble path this process can be made to cease. Hence unlike the worldling he is not caught unawares in the net of conceptual proliferation, but applies his energy to the work of cutting the tangles that keep him from his imminent freedom.

Nevertheless, the learner is urged by the Buddha to refrain from conceiving and delight: "Let him not conceive (himself as) earth; let him not conceive (himself) in earth; let him not conceive (himself apart) from earth; let him not conceive 'earth is mine'; let him not delight in earth." The reason for this injunction is that a remnant of the dispositions to conceiving and delight persist in the learner's mental constitution. He has eradicated the tendency to views and so can no longer be assailed by the conceivings that arise on this account. But he has only weakened, not yet extirpated, the defilements of craving and conceit, and therefore remains vulnerable to the conceivings which arise through these motives. At times, even, when he allows his mindfulness to slacken, he may still indulge in thoughts of "I" and "mine," though he can never permit these to harden into settled views.

Since personality view *(sakkāyadiṭṭhi)* and the conceit "I am" *(asmimāna)* both revolve around the sense of egohood, the question may arise of the exact relationship between the two; in particular, it may be asked how conceit can occur in the absence of any view of a self in the five aggregates. These issues are raised and explained by the bhikkhu Khemaka in a sutta bearing his name. The Venerable Khemaka, a non-returner, was asked by a group of bhikkhus how he could rid himself of a view of self without yet being an arahat.

To their inquiries the Venerable Khemaka replied (SN 22:89/S III 130):

> I do not say "I am" *(asmi)* in regard to material form, feeling, perception, mental formations, or consciousness, nor do I say that there is an "I am" apart from material form, feeling, perception, mental formations, and consciousness. However, a sense that "I am" is still found in me in reference to the five clinging aggregates; but I do not consider "this I am" *(ayam aham asmi).* ... Even though the ariyan disciple has abandoned the five lower fetters (making him a non-returner), nevertheless a residual conceit "I am" *(anusahagato asmī ti māno),* desire "I am" *(asmī ti chando),* and latent tendency "I am" *(asmī ti anusayo)* still remains in him in reference to the five clinging aggregates.

The idea "I am" is a spontaneous, non-thematic notion born from the basic unawareness of the egoless nature of phenomena. It becomes manifest in consciousness in a dual form—as a conceit or wrong estimation of oneself in relation to actuality and as a desire directed towards the perpetuation of one's being. Both these forms are in essence pre-reflective. Though often reinforced by later reflection, they do not require it, but can subsist in its absence as well as in its presence. The view of a self, on the other hand, is a thematic consideration bound up with reflectivity as an inherent part of its structure. Even when held dogmatically or accepted in faith without examination, it involves at least a modicum of deliberation precipitating a doctrinal stance as its articulated product. The basis for deliberation is the original notion of egoity, the idea "I am," which evolves into a view of self when the worldling accepts the idea at its face value—as pointing to a real "I"—and attempts to fill in the reference by identifying one or another of the five aggregates as this "I." Such a mistake the learner can no longer make. With his penetration of the teaching he has seen through the illusion of the ego and therefore no longer inclines to seek his identity among the five aggregates. However, so long as a trace of ignorance remains unabolished in the deeper strata of his mental continuum, an attenuated sense of egohood lingers over his experience in the form of a subtle craving and conceit.

For the present, therefore, the Buddha enjoins the learner to refrain from conceiving in order that he may achieve full understanding of the bases. Whereas the uninstructed worldling conceives the aggregates through craving, conceit, and views, as "This is mine, this am I, this is my self," the learner knows to reverse this mode of consideration. Applying his direct knowledge to the aggregates, he contemplates them thus: "This is not mine, this am I not, this is not my self" *(n'etaṃ mama, n'eso'ham asmi, na m'eso attā).* By the first he attenuates craving, by the second he attenuates conceit; the third, useful for the neophyte in training, for the learner serves merely to confirm his freedom from a view of self. As he persists in his practice of contemplation, his insight gradually develops to maturity, until he eliminates the last traces of ignorance, and with them, the conceivings of subjectivity sprung from craving and conceit.

## The Arahat

The third expository section of the sutta describes the cognitive pattern of the arahat, the liberated one. Both the learner and the arahat share in the personal realization of the Dhamma. The difference between them consists in the degree to which this realization has penetrated the structure of subjectivity. The Buddha explains the difference as follows (MN 35.24/M I 235):

> Herein, a disciple of mine (i.e., a learner) sees as it really is all material form, feeling, perception, mental formations, and consciousness, thus: "This is not mine, this am I not, this is not my self." To this extent my disciple is one who follows my instructions and exhortation, has crossed over doubt, gotten rid of questioning, attained to self-confidence, and dwells independent of others in the dispensation of the Teacher.
>
> Herein, a bhikkhu, having seen as it really is all material form, etc., thus: "This is not mine, this am I not, this is not my self," is emancipated through non-clinging. To this extent a bhikkhu is an arahat, a cankerless one. … who is emancipated by final knowledge.

For the learner, the penetration of subjectivity is only partial. He has removed the inclination to erroneous views of self, but still must strive to eradicate egoistic clinging in its more subtle forms. But for the arahat, the penetration is complete. He has destroyed the defilements in all degrees, and thus is free from even the slightest propensity to self-affirmation. The bases of cognition have been fully understood, ignorance has been abandoned root and branch, and craving, conceit, and views have been brought to their final end.

The arahat, therefore, no longer conceives anything in any way. He does not conceive the datum, he does not conceive in the datum, he does not conceive from the datum, he does not conceive the datum as "mine." This does not mean that the arahat has ceased to cognize. His cognitive apparatus continues to function with full efficiency, even more subtle and sensitive than it was prior to his attainment. But now it simply registers the impinging phenomena as they appear, without distortion or falsification. The arahat no longer sees pleasant objects as attractive, for he is free from lust; he no longer sees unpleasant objects as repulsive, for he is free from hatred; he no longer sees neutral objects as confusing, for he is free from delusion. He does not add and does not take away. Whatever presents itself, presents itself just as it is. It is seen in its bare actuality, shorn of all embellishments and conceptual proliferations. For him there is in the seen only the seen, in the heard only the heard, in the sensed only the sensed, in the cognized only the cognized. There is no notion that "I see, I hear, I sense, I cognize," no notion that the seen, heard, sensed, and cognized are "mine."

To be sure, the arahat is at perfect liberty to make use of such terms and designations as "I" and "mine." Freedom from the bondage of concepts does not imply a stricture prohibiting their use. But the arahat deploys them only as expedients for the purpose of communication. He is no longer deceived by them; he no longer takes them as springs to unjustified assumptions. He sees them as convenient expressions, not as labels for substantial realities. He may say "This is my robe," but he is aware that the "my" arises only through a convention of use and not as an indicator for a real owner. In his own thoughts there is only "this robe to be worn over this body." He may say "I am going to the village," but he knows that there is no agent who goes, only a procession of aggregates involved in the act of going.

Because he has eliminated conceiving, the arahat no longer seeks delight in the objects he encounters. He no longer pursues them in the hope of pleasure and enjoyment. In the absence of delight there is no condition for the renewal of *saṃsāric* existence. Thus, with the exhaustion of his present life, the arahat brings the long, long round to a close. He has reached the end of birth, ageing, and death, and with it, the end of suffering.

## The Tathāgata

Like the arahat, the Buddha also has attained the destruction of defilements, and therefore his own cognitive pattern, as shown in the next section, is fundamentally the same as the arahat's. He directly knows each of the cognitive bases as it really is, and no longer conceives them since he has eliminated craving, conceit, and views. His stature surpasses that of the arahat-disciple in two principal respects, one concerning the range of his understanding, the other the priority of his attainment.

The first is indicated by a slight change occurring in the first expository passage of the "Tathāgata" section. Whereas the arahat-disciple does not conceive phenomena simply because he has fully understood them *(pariññātaṃ),* the Buddha does not conceive them because he has fully understood them to the end *(pariññātantaṃ).* This slight alteration, as the commentary explains, points to the difference in the respective ranges of the knowledge of disciples and the Buddha. The disciples can reach emancipation by comprehending a limited segment of knowable phenomena, but the Buddha reaches emancipation through the knowledge of omniscience *(sabbaññutañāṇa).* He knows whatever can be known in all its modes and relations; there is nothing which escapes the net of his faculty of comprehension. It is this knowledge which makes him properly a perfectly enlightened Buddha *(sammāsambuddha),* with the authority to found a dispensation and the capacity to enlighten others.

The second difference between disciples and the Buddha concerns the order of their attainments. The disciple achieves deliverance in dependence upon the Buddha, but the Buddha attains enlightenment without a teacher or guide, entirely through his own self-evolved wisdom. His knowledge is not received via a course of transmission, as is the disciple's, but flares up in the darkness of ignorance out of his individual application to the right investigation of phenomena. This aspect of the Buddha's enlightenment is implied by the second expository passage of the "Tathāgata" section, discussing the Buddha's realization of dependent origination—the unique content of his enlightenment discovered by him as he sat in meditation beneath the Bodhi Tree.

The insertion of the chain of conditions at this point in the sutta serves the further purpose of linking up the main thread of the discourse with the two central pillars of the Buddha's teaching—the doctrine of dependent origination and the Four Noble Truths. The first expository section traced the cognitive process of the worldling, underlined by latent ignorance, from the stage of perverted perception, through the various modes of conceiving, to delight in the bases of cognition. Now, by stating that "delight is the root of suffering" and continuing through the subsequent factors in the originative chain, the Buddha spells out the consequences of conceiving and delight. Conceiving and delight are the origin of suffering, and when they are yielded to, will produce their inevitable result: birth issuing in new ageing, sickness, and death, and these bringing the secondary forms of suffering in their trail. The antidote to this originative process lies, as the sutta shows, precisely in the penetration of its own inner system of dynamics. For when the springs of origination are detected and exposed, they are drained of their potential for causation and cease to give rise to their usual effects. Ignorance is transformed into knowledge, craving is extinguished by dispassion, and the round of existence is thereby terminated so that it can never be set rolling again. Thus the Buddha brings the discourse to its conclusion with the triumphant proclamation of his own supreme enlightenment—the great awakening which has extricated with utmost finality the buried root of *saṃsāric* existence.

## Conclusion

At the conclusion of the discourse, the sutta states that the bhikkhus did *not* delight in the words of the Exalted One. This is a direct inversion of the almost invariable formula closing a sutta, which runs: "Elated in mind, the bhikkhus delighted in the words of the Exalted One." Its occurrence, therefore, is a cause for conjecture. The commentary explains this peculiar ending by reference to the Buddha's original purpose in expounding the Mūlapariyāya Sutta: to shatter the conceit of the five hundred bhikkhus who, out of intellectual pride, had become negligent in their religious duties. Because these bhikkhus could not understand such an abstruse discourse, their minds were perplexed and their pride broken. On account of their confusion they did not delight in the Master's words.

Although this exegetical tradition is certainly plausible, another explanation for the Mūlapariyāya Sutta's unique ending is possible as well. The commentary tells us that before their ordination as monks in the Buddha's dispensation, these bhikkhus were brahmins who had achieved mastery over the Vedas. It may be suggested that the reason for their displeasure was not their inability to understand the Buddha's discourse, but rather the fact that they understood it too well. For their brahminical predilections may have carried through past their conversion to the doctrine of the Buddha, and wrongly influenced their understanding of the Dhamma in ways they were not ready to renounce. The pivot of their wrong understanding most likely would have been the belief in a permanent immortal self, the Ātman, a cardinal tenet of brahminic philosophy and a key target of the Buddha's exposition in the sutta. A well-known passage in the Bṛhadāraṇyaka Upaniṣad (BĀU 3.7.3ff.) presents a striking parallel to the flexional pattern of conceivings given in the present discourse:

> He who inhabits the earth, yet is within the earth, whom the earth does not know, whose body the earth is, and who controls the earth from within—he is your Self, the Inner Controller, the Immortal.

Other phenomena similarly treated are: water, fire, sky, air, heaven, the sun, the quarters, the moon and stars, space, darkness, light, beings, breath, speech, eye, ear, mind, skin, intellect, and organs of generation. In exposing such modes of thought as mere conceivings of the uninstructed worldling, the Buddha may have struck at the heart of these bhikkhus' residual brahminic convictions, thereby provoking their resentment.

Nevertheless, the commentary relates a happy outcome to the entire course of events. After hearing the Mūlapariyāya Sutta, the five hundred bhikkhus became humble and respectful. They resumed their religious duties, such as regularly attending upon the Buddha and going to listen to his explanations of the Dhamma. At a later time, when he knew that their spiritual faculties had matured and their understanding deepened, the Buddha expounded to these same bhikkhus the Gotamaka Sutta (AN 3:123/A I 276), proclaiming the excellent qualifications of the Exalted One, his teaching, and his order of disciples. As a result of listening to this sutta, all five hundred bhikkhus became liberated from defilements and brought their spiritual training to completion with the realization of final emancipation.

# APPENDIX

## A SCHEMATIC REPRESENTATION OF THE MŪLAPARIYĀYA SUTTA

(X = any of the twent-four bases)

| *Individual* | *Primary Cognition** | *Initial Response* | *Conceptual Response* | *Emotive Response* | *Reason* |
|---|---|---|---|---|---|
| the uninstructed worldling | perceives X | perceives X as X | conceives X<br>conceives in X<br>conceives from X<br>conceives "X is mine" | delights in X | because he has not fully understood X |
| the learner | perceives X | directly knows X | open, therefore:<br>let him not conceive X<br>let him not conceive in X<br>let him not conceive from X<br>let him not conceive "X is mine" | open, therefore: let him not delight in X | in order that he might fully understand X |
| the Arahat | perceives X | directly knows X | does not conceive X<br>does not conceive in X<br>does not conceive from X<br>does not conceive "X is mine" | does not delight in X | because he has fully understood X<br>because he is devoid of lust<br>because he is devoid of hate<br>because he is devoid of delusion |
| the Buddha | perceives X | directly knows X | does not conceive X<br>does not conceive in X<br>does not conceive from X<br>does not conceive "X is mine" | does not delight in X | because he has fully understood X to the end<br>because he has understood dependent origination |

* Not explicitly mentioned in Sutta.

# Part One
# Mūlapariyāya Sutta

## The Discourse on the Root of Existence

### (Introductory)

1. Thus have I heard. On one occasion the Exalted One was dwelling at Ukkaṭṭhā, at the foot of a royal Sāla tree in the Subhaga Grove. There the Exalted One addressed the bhikkhus: "Bhikkhus." "Lord," the bhikkhus replied. The Exalted One said: "I will teach you, bhikkhus, the exposition of the root of all things. Listen and attend carefully to what I shall say." "Yes, Lord," they replied. The Exalted One spoke.

### The Worldling

2. "Herein, bhikkhus, an uninstructed worldling, who is without regard for the ariyans, unskilled in the Dhamma of the ariyans, undisciplined in the Dhamma of the ariyans, who is without regard for the good men, unskilled in the Dhamma of the good men, undisciplined in the Dhamma of the good men—he perceives earth as earth. Having perceived earth as earth, he conceives (himself as) earth; he conceives (himself) in earth; he conceives (himself apart) from earth; he conceives 'earth is mine'; he delights in earth. What is the reason? Because it has not been fully understood by him, I declare.

"He perceives water as water. Having perceived water as water, he conceives (himself as) water; he conceives (himself) in water; he conceives (himself apart) from water; he conceives 'water is mine'; he delights in water. What is the reason? Because it has not been fully understood by him, I declare.

"He perceives fire as fire. Having perceived fire as fire, he conceives (himself as) fire; he conceives (himself) in fire; he conceives (himself apart) from fire; he conceives 'fire is mine'; he delights in fire. What is the reason? Because it has not been fully understood by him, I declare.

"He perceives air as air. Having perceived air as air, he conceives (himself as) air; he conceives (himself) in air; he conceives (himself apart) from air; he conceives 'air is mine'; he delights in air. What is the reason? Because it has not been fully understood by him, I declare.

3. "He perceives beings as beings. Having perceived beings as beings, he conceives beings; he conceives (himself) in beings; he conceives (himself apart) from beings; he conceives 'beings are mine'; he delights in beings. What is the reason? Because they have not been fully understood by him, I declare.

"He perceives gods as gods. Having perceived gods as gods, he conceives gods; he conceives (himself) in gods; he conceives (himself apart) from gods; he conceives 'gods are mine'; he delights in gods. What is the reason? Because they have not been fully understood by him, I declare.

"He perceives Pajāpati as Pajāpati.[9] Having perceived Pajāpati as Pajāpati, he conceives Pajāpati; he conceives (himself) in Pajāpati; he conceives (himself apart) from Pajāpati; he conceives 'Pajāpati is mine'; he delights in Pajāpati. What is the reason? Because it has not been fully understood by him, I declare.

"He perceives Brahmā as Brahmā. Having perceived Brahmā as Brahmā, he conceives Brahmā; he conceives (himself) in Brahmā; he conceives (himself apart) from Brahmā; he conceives 'Brahmā is mine'; he delights in Brahmā. What is the reason? Because it has not been fully understood by him, I declare.

"He perceives the gods of Streaming Radiance *(ābhassarā)* as the gods of Streaming Radiance. Having perceived the gods of Streaming Radiance as the gods of Streaming Radiance, he conceives the gods of Streaming Radiance; he conceives (himself) in the gods of Streaming Radiance; he conceives (himself apart) from the gods of Streaming Radiance; he conceives 'the gods of Streaming Radiance are mine'; he delights in the gods of Streaming Radiance.

What is the reason? Because they have not been fully understood by him, I declare.

"He perceives the gods of Refulgent Glory *(subhakiṇhā)* as the gods of Refulgent Glory. Having perceived the gods of Refulgent Glory as the gods of Refulgent Glory, he conceives the gods of Refulgent Glory; he conceives (himself) in the gods of Refulgent Glory; he conceives (himself apart) from the gods of Refulgent Glory; he conceives 'the gods of Refulgent Glory are mine'; he delights in the gods of Refulgent Glory. What is the reason? Because they have not been fully understood by him, I declare.

"He perceives the gods of Abundant Fruit *(vehapphalā)* as the gods of Abundant Fruit. Having perceived the gods of Abundant Fruit as the gods of Abundant Fruit, he conceives the gods of Abundant Fruit; he conceives (himself) in the gods of Abundant Fruit; he conceives (himself apart) from the gods of Abundant Fruit; he conceives 'the gods of Abundant Fruit are mine'; he delights in the gods of Abundant Fruit. What is the reason? Because they have not been fully understood by him, I declare.

"He perceives the Vanquisher *(abhibhū)* as the Vanquisher. Having perceived the Vanquisher as the Vanquisher, he conceives the Vanquisher; he conceives (himself) in the Vanquisher; he conceives (himself apart) from the Vanquisher; he conceives 'the Vanquisher is mine'; he delights in the Vanquisher. What is the reason? Because it has not been fully understood by him, I declare.

4. "He perceives the base of infinite space as the base of infinite space. Having perceived the base of infinite space as the base of infinite space, he conceives (himself as) the base of infinite space; he conceives (himself) in the base of infinite space; he conceives (himself apart) from the base of infinite space; he conceives 'the base of infinite space is mine'; he delights in the base of infinite space. What is the reason? Because it has not been fully understood by him, I declare.

"He perceives the base of infinite consciousness as the base of infinite consciousness. Having perceived the base of infinite consciousness as the base of infinite consciousness, he conceives (himself as) the base of infinite consciousness; he conceives (himself) in the base of infinite consciousness; he conceives (himself apart) from the base of infinite consciousness; he conceives 'the base of infinite consciousness is mine'; he delights in the base of infinite consciousness. What is the reason? Because it has not been fully understood by him, I declare.

"He perceives the base of nothingness as the base of nothingness. Having perceived the base of nothingness as the base of nothingness, he conceives (himself as) the base of nothingness; he conceives (himself) in the base of nothingness; he conceives (himself apart) from the base of nothingness; he conceives 'the base of nothingness is mine'; he delights in the base of nothingness. What is the reason? Because it has not been fully understood by him, I declare.

"He perceives the base of neither perception nor non-perception as the base of neither perception nor non-perception. Having perceived the base of neither perception nor non-perception as the base of neither perception nor non-perception, he conceives (himself as) the base of neither perception nor non-perception; he conceives (himself) in the base of neither perception nor non-perception; he conceives (himself apart) from the base of neither perception nor non-perception; he conceives 'the base of neither perception nor non-perception is mine'; he delights in the base of neither perception nor non-perception. What is the reason? Because it has not been fully understood by him, I declare.

5. "He perceives the seen as the seen. Having perceived the seen as the seen, he conceives (himself as) the seen; he conceives (himself) in the seen; he conceives (himself apart) from the seen; he conceives 'the seen is mine'; he delights in the seen. What is the reason? Because it has not been fully understood by him, I declare.

"He perceives the heard as the heard. Having perceived the heard as the heard, he conceives (himself as) the heard; he conceives (himself) in the heard; he conceives (himself apart) from the heard; he conceives 'the heard is mine'; he delights in the heard. What is the reason? Because it has not been fully understood by him, I declare.

"He perceives the sensed as the sensed. Having perceived the sensed as the sensed, he conceives (himself as) the sensed; he conceives (himself) in the sensed; he conceives (himself apart) from the sensed; he conceives 'the sensed is mine'; he delights in the sensed. What is the reason? Because it has not been fully understood by him, I declare.

"He perceives the cognized as the cognized. Having perceived the cognized as the cognized, he conceives (himself as) the cognized; he conceives (himself) in the cognized; he conceives (himself apart) from the cognized; he conceives 'the cognized is mine'; he delights in the cognized. What is the reason? Because it has not been fully understood by him, I declare.

6. "He perceives unity as unity. Having perceived unity as unity, he conceives (himself as) unity; he conceives (himself) in unity; he conceives (himself apart) from unity; he conceives 'unity is mine'; he delights in unity. What is the reason? Because it has not been fully understood by him, I declare.

"He perceives diversity as diversity. Having perceived diversity as diversity, he conceives (himself as) diversity; he conceives (himself) in diversity; he conceives (himself apart) from diversity; he conceives 'diversity is mine'; he delights in diversity. What is the reason? Because it has not been fully understood by him, I declare.

"He perceives all as all. Having perceived all as all, he conceives (himself as) all; he conceives (himself) in all; he conceives (himself apart) from all; he conceives 'all is mine'; he delights in all. What is the reason? Because it has not been fully understood by him, I declare.

"He perceives nibbāna as nibbāna. Having perceived nibbāna as nibbāna, he conceives (himself as) nibbāna; he conceives (himself) in nibbāna; he conceives (himself apart) from nibbāna; he conceives 'nibbāna is mine'; he delights in nibbāna. What is the reason? Because it has not been fully understood by him, I declare.

## The Learner

7. "A bhikkhu who is a learner, bhikkhus, who has not attained his heart's ideal but is still yearning for the supreme security from bondage—he directly knows earth as earth. Having directly known earth as earth, let him not conceive (himself as) earth; let him not

conceive (himself) in earth; let him not conceive (himself apart) from earth; let him not conceive 'earth is mine'; let him not delight in earth. What is the reason? Because it should be fully understood by him, I declare.

"He directly knows water as water ... *(the same pattern is repeated down to)* ... He directly knows nibbāna as nibbāna. Having directly known nibbāna as nibbāna, let him not conceive (himself as) nibbāna; let him not conceive (himself) in nibbāna; let him not conceive (himself apart) from nibbāna; let him not conceive 'nibbāna is mine'; let him not delight in nibbāna. What is the reason? Because it should be fully understood by him, I declare.

## The Arahat

### I

8. "A bhikkhu who is an arahat, bhikkhus, a cankerless one, who has lived the holy life, done what had to be done, laid down the burden, attained his own goal, eliminated the fetters of existence, and is emancipated through final knowledge—he directly knows earth as earth. Having directly known earth as earth, he does not conceive (himself as) earth; he does not conceive (himself) in earth; he does not conceive (himself apart) from earth; he does not conceive 'earth is mine'; he does not delight in earth. What is the reason? Because it has been fully understood by him, I declare.

"He directly knows water as water ... *(the same pattern is repeated down to)* ... He directly knows nibbāna as nibbāna. Having directly known nibbāna as nibbāna, he does not conceive (himself as) nibbāna; he does not conceive (himself) in nibbāna; he does not conceive (himself apart) from nibbāna; he does not conceive 'nibbāna is mine'; he does not delight in nibbāna. What is the reason? Because it has been fully understood by him, I declare.

### II

9. "A bhikkhu who is an arahat, bhikkhus, ... emancipated through final knowledge—he directly knows earth as earth. Having directly known earth as earth, he does not conceive (himself as) earth; he does not conceive (himself) in earth; he does not conceive (himself

apart) from earth; he does not conceive 'earth is mine'; he does not delight in earth. What is the reason? Because he is devoid of lust through the destruction of lust.

"He directly knows water as water ... nibbāna as nibbāna. ... What is the reason? Because he is devoid of lust through the destruction of lust.

III

10. "A bhikkhu who is an arahat, bhikkhus, ... emancipated through final knowledge—he directly knows earth as earth. Having directly known earth as earth, he does not conceive (himself as) earth; he does not conceive (himself) in earth; he does not conceive (himself apart) from earth; he does not conceive 'earth is mine'; he does not delight in earth. What is the reason? Because he is devoid of hate through the destruction of hate.

"He directly knows water as water ... nibbāna as nibbāna. ... What is the reason? Because he is devoid of hate through the destruction of hate.

IV

11. "A bhikkhu who is an arahat, bhikkhus, ... emancipated through final knowledge—he directly knows earth as earth. Having directly known earth as earth, he does not conceive (himself as) earth: he does not conceive (himself) in earth; he does not conceive (himself apart) from earth; he does not conceive 'earth is mine'; he does not delight in earth. What is the reason? Because he is devoid of delusion through the destruction of delusion.

"He directly knows water as water ... nibbāna as nibbāna. ... What is the reason? Because he is devoid of delusion through the destruction of delusion.

## The Tathāgata

I

12. "The Tathāgata, bhikkhus, the arahat, the perfectly enlightened Buddha, directly knows earth as earth. Having directly known earth as earth, he does not conceive (himself as) earth; he does not conceive

(himself) in earth; he does not conceive (himself apart) from earth; he does not conceive 'earth is mine'; he does not delight in earth. What is the reason? Because it has been fully understood to the end by the Tathāgata, I declare.

"He directly knows water as water … nibbāna as nibbāna. … What is the reason? Because it has been fully understood to the end by the Tathāgata, I declare.

II

13. "The Tathāgata, bhikkhus, the arahat, the perfectly enlightened Buddha, directly knows earth as earth. Having directly known earth as earth, he does not conceive (himself as) earth; he does not conceive (himself) in earth; he does not conceive (himself apart) from earth; he does not conceive 'earth is mine'; he does not delight in earth. What is the reason? Because he has understood that delight is the root of suffering, and that with existence (as condition) there is birth, and that for what has come to be there is ageing and death. Therefore, bhikkhus, through the complete destruction, fading away, cessation, abandoning, and relinquishing of all cravings, the Tathāgata has awakened to the supreme perfect enlightenment, I declare.

"He directly knows water as water … nibbāna as nibbāna. … What is the reason? Because he has understood that delight is the root of suffering, and that with existence (as condition) there is birth, and that for what has come to be there is ageing and death. Therefore, bhikkhus, through the complete destruction, fading away, cessation, abandoning, and relinquishing of all cravings, the Tathāgata has awakened to the supreme perfect enlightenment, I declare."

Thus spoke the Exalted One. But those bhikkhus did *not* delight in the word of the Exalted One.[10]

# Part Two

# The Commentarial Exegesis of the Mūlapariyāya Sutta

## 1. Introductory Section

**Cy.** Since this commentary will be clearer if we first examine the grounds on which the Exalted One delivers a sutta, we will deal with this matter first.

### *(The four grounds for the delivery of a sutta [suttanikkhepa])*

There are four grounds for the delivery of a sutta: (1) personal inclination *(attajjhāsaya),* (2) the inclination of others *(parajjhāsaya),* (3) the proposal of a question *(pucchāvasika),* and (4) the occurrence of a special incident *(aṭṭhuppattika).*

Among these, (1) those suttas which the Exalted One declares entirely through his own inclination, without being requested by others, have personal inclination as the ground for their delivery. Some examples of this class are the Ākaṅkheyya Sutta (MN 6), the Vattha Sutta (MN 7), the Mahāsatipaṭṭhāna Sutta (DN 22), the Mahāsaḷāyatanavibhaṅga Sutta (MN 137), the Ariyavaṃsa Sutta (AN 4:28), and many suttas on the right endeavours, the bases of spiritual success, the faculties, powers, factors of enlightenment, and factors of the path.

(2) Those suttas which he declares by reason of the inclinations of others, after discerning their inclination, acquiescence, state of mind, aspiration, and capacity for understanding, have the inclinations of others as the ground for their delivery. An instance is the case of Rāhula, when the Exalted One, perceiving that the factors maturing towards emancipation had reached maturity in Rāhula,

thought: "Let me now lead Rāhula to the destruction of the cankers." (MN 147.1) Some suttas of this class are the Cūḷarāhula Sutta (MN 147), the Mahārāhula Sutta (MN 62), the Dhammacakkappavattana Sutta (SN 56:11), and the Dhātuvibhaṅga Sutta (MN 140).

(3) When the four assemblies, the four classes, *nāgas, supaṇṇas, gandhabbas, asuras, yakkhas,*[11] the gods of the sense-sphere-heavens, and *Mahābrahmās* approach the Exalted One and ask questions—about the factors of enlightenment, hindrances, clinging-aggregates, the "best treasure of man," and so on—and the Exalted One speaks a sutta in reply, those suttas have the proposal of a question as the ground for their delivery. To this class belong numerous suttas of the Saṃyutta Nikāya (e.g., SN 1:1), and the Sakkapañhā (DN 21), Cūḷavedalla (MN 44), Mahāvedalla (MN 43), Sāmaññaphala (DN 2), and other suttas.

(4) And those suttas declared because a special incident has occurred, these have the occurrence of a special incident as the ground for their pronouncement. Examples are the Dhammadāyāda (MN 3), Cūḷasīhanāda (MN 11), the Candūpama (SN 16:3), Puttamaṃsūpama (SN 12:63), Dārakkhandhūpama (SN 35:241), Aggikkhandhūpama (AN 7:68, SN 12:52), Pheṇapiṇḍūpama (SN 22:95), and Păricchattakūpama Suttas (AN 7:65).

Of these four, this sutta has the occurrence of a special incident as the ground for its delivery, since it was delivered by the Exalted One on account of the occurrence of a special incident. And what was that incident? The arising of conceit on account of learning. For, it is told, five hundred brahmins who were masters of the three Vedas heard the Exalted One teaching the Dhamma, and recognizing the danger in sense pleasures and the benefit in renunciation, went forth into homelessness in his presence. In no long time they mastered the entire word of the Buddha, and on account of their learning gave rise to conceit. "Whatever the Exalted One says," they thought, "that we quickly understand. The Exalted One does not say anything which does not come within scope of the three genders, the four kinds of terms, and the seven declensions.[12] Thus there is nothing in what he says that presents a knotty problem to us." As a result they neglected to show proper reverence for the Exalted One, rarely going to attend upon him or to listen to him teach the Dhamma. The Exalted One understood the course their minds were taking, and aware that it would not be possible for them to realize the path or the fruit so long as the pillar of conceit was not uprooted from their minds, he made their conceit the occasion for the delivery of a sutta. Skillful in teaching, he undertook this teaching on "the exposition of the root of all things" for the purpose of shattering their conceit.

### "The Exposition of the Root of All Things" (*sabbadhammamūlapariyāya*)

**Cy.** "Of all" means without exception *(anavasesa).* For the word "all" expresses the lack of an exception, and signifies the lack of an exception in whatever term it comes into connection with.

**Sub. Cy.** The word "all" is found to be applied to four cases: the all-inclusive all *(sabbasabba),* the all of restricted reference *(padesasabba),* the all of the sense bases *(āyatanasabba),* and the all of personality *(sakkāyasabba).* Thus, in the passage: "All dhammas in all their modes enter the threshold of the Exalted One's portal of knowledge" (Nidd I 357), the all-inclusive all is intended. In the passage: "You have all spoken well, Sāriputta" (MN 32.17/M I 219), it is the all of restricted reference. In the passage: "I will teach you the all, bhikkhus. The eye and visible forms ... the mind and mental objects" (SN 35:23/S IV 15), it is the all of the sense bases. And in the passage: "He perceives all as all" (MN 1.25/M I 3), it is the all of personality. Among these four, the all-inclusive all has unrestricted application, the other three restricted application. In the present case, the all of personality is meant.[13]

**Cy.** The word "dhamma" is found used in the following senses: the scriptures *(pariyatti),* the (Four Noble) Truths *(sacca),* concentration *(samādhi),* wisdom *(paññā),* nature *(pakati),* things endowed with a specific nature *(sabhāva),* emptiness *(suññatā),* merit *(puñña),* a disciplinary offense *(āpatti),* the knowable *(ñeyya),* etc. In the passage: "Herein, a bhikkhu masters the Dhamma—the suttas, songs," etc. (MN 22.11/M I 134) it occurs in the sense of the scriptures. "He saw the Dhamma, understood the Dhamma" (DN 3.2.22/D I 110)—in the sense of the (Four Noble) Truths. "Those Exalted Ones were of such dhammas" (DN 28.1/D III 100)—concentration.

"Truth, dhamma, fortitude, generosity" (Sn 188)— wisdom. "Of a nature to be born, of a nature to grow old, of a nature to die" (DN 22.18/D II 307)—nature. "Wholesome dhammas" (Dhs Mātikā 1/ Dhs 1)—things endowed with a specific nature. "On that occasion there are dhammas" (Dhs §121/Dhs 25)—emptiness. "Dhamma well-practised issues in bliss" (Sn 182)—merit. "Two dhammas are unfixed" (SVibh Aniyata intro./Vin III 194)—a disciplinary offense. And in the passage: "All dhammas in all their modes enter the threshold of the Exalted One's portal of knowledge," it is the knowable. Here the word occurs in the sense of things endowed with a specific nature. This is the word-meaning: "They bear their own characteristics, thus they are dhammas" *(attano lakkhaṇaṃ dhārentī ti dhammā).*

**Sub. Cy.** "They bear their own characteristics": although there are no dhammas devoid of their own characteristics, this is still said for the purpose of showing that these are mere dhammas endowed with their specific natures devoid of such attributions as that of a "being," etc. Whereas such entities as self, beauty, pleasurableness, and permanence, etc., or nature *(pakati),* substance *(dabba),* soul *(jīva),* body, etc., which are mere misconstructions *(parikappitākāramatta)* due to craving and views, or such entities as "sky-flowers," etc., which are mere expressions of conventional discourse *(lokavohāramatta),* cannot be discovered as ultimately real actualities *(saccikaṭṭhaparamatthato),* these dhammas (i.e., those endowed with a specific nature) can. These dhammas are discovered as ultimately real actualities. And though there is no real distinction (between these dhammas and their characteristics), still, in order to facilitate understanding, the exposition makes a distinction as a mere metaphorical device *(upacāramatta).*[14] Or else they are borne, they are discerned, known, according to their specific nature, thus they are dhammas *(dhārīyanti vā yathāsabhāvato avadhāriyanti ñāyantī ti dhammā).*

**Cy.** The word "root" *(mūla)* here means particular root-cause *(asādhāraṇahetu).*

**Sub. Cy.** The meaning is: the unique condition for each of the dhammas included in personality. And what is that? Craving, conceit, and views, or ignorance, etc.[15] For just as the conceivings of craving, (conceit, and views), which arise in reference to the bases of conceiving such as earth, etc., are the root-cause for their occurrence, so also is ignorance, etc. Thus it is said below (in the sutta), in conformity with this: "The uninstructed worldling," etc., "Because it is not fully understood by him," and "Delight is the root of suffering"; and in addition, "Because he is devoid of lust, hate, and delusion." Hence their functioning as root-causes is shown.

**Cy.** The word *pariyāya* occurs in the texts in the sense of teaching *(desanā)*, cause *(kāraṇa)*, and turn *(vāra)*. Here it has the meaning of teaching and cause. Thus the phrase "the exposition of the root of all things" signifies the cause designated the particular root-cause of all things, or the teaching of the cause of all things. But this sutta has to be carefully interpreted. It is not all specific natured dhammas of the four planes that is indicated by the words "all things," but only all dhammas pertaining to the three planes included in personality *(sakkāyapariyāpannā pana tebhūmakā dhammā va)*.[16] This here is the purport.

**Sub. Cy.** The purport is: all the dhammas beginning with earth which function as the bases for conceiving *(maññanāvatthu)*.

### "An uninstructed worldling" (*assutavā puthujjana*)

**Cy.** Herein, he is uninstructed, needs to be taught, because he possesses neither learning *(āgama)* nor spiritual achievement *(adhigama)*. For he who possesses neither the learning running counter to the activity of conceiving because he has neglected to study, question, and discriminate the aggregates, elements, sense bases, truths, law of conditionality, and foundations of mindfulness, etc., nor spiritual achievements because he has failed to achieve what should be achieved by practice, is said to be "uninstructed" on account of his deficiency in learning and spiritual achievement. He is one who needs to be taught.

He is called a worldling for such reasons
As that he generates a multitude of things,
Because he is immersed in the herd,
And because he is a person who is distinct.

The worldling is so-called because he generates a multitude of diverse defilements, etc.[17] As it is said: "They generate a multitude of defilements, hence they are worldlings. They have not destroyed the multiple forms of personality view, they look up to a multitude of teachers, they have not emerged from the multitude of destinations, they form multiple kamma-formations, they are swept away by a multitude of floods, afflicted by a multitude of afflictions, consumed by a multitude of fevers—hence they are worldlings. They are lustful and greedy for the five multiple strands of sense pleasure; therein they are bound, infatuated, addicted, attached, fastened, and confined—hence they are worldlings. They are obstructed, hindered, and enveloped by the five multiple hindrances; there they are enclosed, concealed, and incarcerated—hence they are worldlings" (Nidd I 249). Again, one who is included among the incalculable multitude of people who live according to an inferior doctrine and are averse to the doctrine of the ariyans is called a worldling. And a person distinct or remote from the ariyans endowed with such noble qualities as virtue, learning, etc., is called a worldling. Between the two types of worldlings mentioned in the following verse it is the blind worldling who is called the "uninstructed worldling."

> The Enlightened One, the Kinsman of the Sun,
> Speaks of the worldling in a twofold way.
> One is the worldling blinded by darkness,
> The other the worldling noble and good.

### "Who is without regard for the ariyans"

**Cy.** The ariyans are so-called because they are remote from the defilements, because they are not heading towards decline, because they are heading towards growth, and because they are worthy of being honoured by the world together with its gods.[18] Buddhas, paccekabuddhas, and disciples of the Buddhas are called "ariyans." Or the Buddhas alone are called "ariyans" here, while the phrase "the good men" applies to paccekabuddhas and disciples as well. Men who shine *(sobhana)* through their possession of supramundane qualities are called 'good men' *(sappurisa).* Or both words apply to all three; that is, Buddhas, paccekabuddhas, and disciples are all both ariyans and good men.

Now, he who by nature has no regard for the ariyans, and does not welcome their sight, is one "who is without regard (lit. without sight) for the ariyans." This type of person is of two kinds: he who does not see them with the eye and he who does not see them with knowledge. And here it is not seeing them with knowledge *(ñāṇena adassāvī)* that is intended. For even though they be seen with the fleshly eye or with the divine eye, they are still unseen, for these eyes apprehend only the outer appearance of the ariyans, not their interior ariyan state. Though dogs, jackals, and others see ariyans with their eyes, they are not seers of the ariyans.

Here is a story to illustrate this: A cankerless elder residing at Cittalapabbata had a personal attendant who had become a monk in old age. One day, after the two had walked for alms, while following the elder carrying the latter's bowl and outer robe, the attendant asked: "Venerable sir, what are the ariyans like?" The elder replied: "Here there is an old man, walking together with an ariyan, doing his duties towards him, carrying his bowl and robe, yet even he does not know what the ariyans are like. So difficult to know are the ariyans, friend." And though this was said, still the attendant didn't get the point.

Thus it is not seeing with the eyes that is meant by the phrase "regard (for the ariyans)," but seeing with knowledge. As it is said: "What is your purpose, Vakkali, in seeing this foul body? He who sees the Dhamma, Vakkali, he sees me" (SN 22:87/S III 120). Therefore, even though one sees the ariyans with one's eyes, so long as one does not see with knowledge the characteristics of impermanence, (suffering, and non-self) seen by the ariyans, and does not achieve the Dhamma achieved by the ariyans, for so long the ariyan state and the qualities constituting an ariyan remain unseen, and one is described as a person "without regard for the ariyans."

## "Unskilled in the Dhamma of the ariyans"

**Cy.** That is, without skill in the ariyan Dhamma classified into the foundations of mindfulness, etc.

### "Undisciplined in the Dhamma of the ariyans"

**Cy.** Here —

The discipline is first twofold,
Each part again divides by five.
Because he lacks in all of this,
He's said to be undisciplined.

This discipline *(vinaya)* is twofold: the discipline of restraint *(saṃvaravinaya)* and the discipline of abandoning *(pahānavinaya)*. And each part of this twofold discipline is again divided into five. The discipline of restraint is fivefold as restraint by virtue *(sīla)*, by mindfulness *(sati)*, by knowledge *(ñāṇa)*, by patience *(khanti)*, and by energy *(viriya)*. Therein, "He is endowed, perfectly endowed, with this restraint of the Pātimokkha" (Vibh §508/Vibh 244)—this is restraint by virtue. "He guards the faculty of the eye, he acquires restraint over the faculty of the eye" (DN 2.64/D I 70)—this is restraint by mindfulness.

Those streams which flow throughout the world, Ajita,
said the Lord,
Mindfulness serves to curb them in,
This I call the restraint of the streams.
But wisdom only turns them off (Sn 1035)—

this (last line) indicates restraint by knowledge. "He patiently endures cold and heat" (MN 2.13/M I 10)—this is restraint by patience. "He does not tolerate an arisen thought of sensual desire, he abandons it" (MN 2.20/M I 11)—this is restraint by energy. This entire (fivefold) restraint is called "restraint" *(saṃvara)* and "discipline" *(vinaya)* because it respectively restrains and disciplines any bodily, (vocal, and mental) misconduct which should be restrained and disciplined. Thus the discipline of restraint is classified as fivefold.

The discipline of abandoning is also fivefold as abandoning by factor-substitution *(tadaṅgappahāna)*, by suppression *(vikkhambhanappahāna)*, by eradication *(samucchedappahāna)*, by subsiding *(paṭipassaddhippahāna)*, and by escape *(nissaraṇappahāna)*. Among these, the abandoning by factor-substitution is the abandoning of a negative factor by the class of insight-knowledge opposed to it, in the same way that darkness is abandoned by the light of a lamp. Thus personality view is abandoned by the defining of mentality-materiality, the views of acausality and wrong causal relationships by the discernment of conditions, uncertainty in regard to this by the subsequent transcending of doubts, the assumption of "I" and "mine" by the insight-comprehension of groups, the perception of the path in what is not the path by the discrimination of the path from what is not the path, annihilationism by the perception of arising, eternalism by the perception of fall, the perception of fearlessness in the fearful by the perception of fear, the perception of satisfaction by the perception of unsatisfactoriness, the perception of delight by the contemplation of disenchantment, the non-desire for release by the knowledge desiring release, non-equanimity by the knowledge of equanimity, running contrary to the structure of things and to nibbāna by conformity-knowledge, and the assumption of the sign of formations by change-of-lineage.[19] This is called "abandoning by factor-substitution."

Abandoning by suppression is the abandonment of the hindrances, etc., by the obstructive power of concentration, either at the level of access *(upacāra)* or absorption *(appanā)*. This is likened to preventing the growth of water-moss by striking the surface of the water with a pot.

Abandoning by eradication is the abandonment of the host of defilements on the side of the origin (of suffering) by completely severing the possibility of their occurrence. It is achieved through the development of the four supramundane paths, and occurs in the individual mental continua of the four individuals attaining to these paths.

The subsiding of the defilements at the four moments of fruition (following the four paths) is the abandoning by subsiding.

Nibbāna, in which all that is conditioned is abandoned by the escape from all that is conditioned, is the abandoning by escape.

Since this entire fivefold abandoning is abandoning in the sense of giving up *(cāga)*, and discipline in the sense of disciplining, it is called the discipline of abandoning. Or else it is called the discipline of abandoning because of the arising of this and that discipline from this or that abandoning. Thus this discipline of abandoning is classified as fivefold.

Because his restraint is repeatedly disrupted and because he has not abandoned what should be abandoned, the uninstructed worldling lacks this discipline that is described briefly as twofold and in detail as tenfold. And lacking it, he is said to be "undisciplined." The same method applies to the corresponding statements in terms of "the good men," for there is no difference in meaning. As it is said; "Those who are ariyans are also good men, and those who are good men are also ariyans. Whether 'the ariyans' is said or 'the good men,' 'the Dhamma of the ariyans' or 'the Dhamma of the good men,' 'the discipline of the ariyans' or 'the discipline of the good men'—these are one, identical, the same, equivalents, interchangeable terms."

Why does the Exalted One, after announcing: "I will teach you, bhikkhus, the exposition of the root of all things," proceed to describe the worldling without even teaching the exposition of the root? In order to show this topic by means of a teaching that has a dhamma as subject and an individual as term of expression.[20] For the teaching of the Buddha is of four kinds: (1) a teaching that has dhammas as subject and dhammas as terms of expression *(dhammādhiṭṭhānā dhammadesanā)*; (2) a teaching that has individuals as subject and dhammas as terms of expression *(dhammādhiṭṭhānā puggaladesanā)*; (3) a teaching that has individuals as subject and individuals as terms of expression *(puggalādhiṭṭhānā puggaladesanā)*; and (4) a teaching that has dhammas as subject and individuals as terms of expression *(puggalādhiṭṭhānā dhammadesanā)*.

Therein, (1) "There are, bhikkhus, these three feelings. What are the three? Pleasant feeling, painful feeling, and neither-pleasant-nor-painful feeling" (SN 36:11/S IV 216)—this is a teaching that has dhammas as subject and dhammas as terms of expression. (2) "This person consists of six elements, six bases of contact, eighteen mental ranges, and four foundations" (MN 140.8/M III 239)—this is a teaching that has individuals as subject and dhammas as terms of expression. (3) "There are, bhikkhus, three kinds of individuals existing in the world. What are the three? The blind, the one-eyed, and the two-eyed" (AN 3:29/A I 128)—this is a teaching that has individuals as subject and individuals as terms of expression. And (4) "What, bhikkhus, is the fear of a bad destination? Herein, bhikkhus, someone reflects: 'The result of bodily misconduct in the life to come is evil' " (AN 4:121/A II 123)—this is a teaching that has dhammas as subject and individuals as terms of expression.

In the present case, since the worldling consists of the bases that have not been fully understood *(puthujjano apariññātavatthuko),* and the conceiving *(maññanā)* that is the root of all the things intended here is itself rooted in lack of full understanding *(apariññāmūlikā),* therefore he describes the worldling first; for when he is introduced, the meaning will be made clear through a teaching that has individuals as terms of expression.

**Sub. Cy.** "The worldling consists of the bases which have not been fully understood"; the aggregates which have not been fully understood through the three kinds of full understanding.[21] For the aggregates are the bases of full understanding.

## 2. The Section on Earth

### "He perceives earth as earth"
### (*paṭhaviṃ paṭhavito sañjānāti*)

**Cy.** Having thus described the worldling, the Master goes on to show his manner of conceiving the bases such as earth, etc., which is the generative source of all the things included in personality. Therein, earth is fourfold: characteristic earth *(lakkhaṇapaṭhavī),* composite earth *(sasambhārapaṭhavī),* objectified earth *(ārammaṇapaṭhavī),* and earth as conventional designation *(sammutipaṭhavī).* (1) In the passage: "What, friends, is the internal earth element? That which is internal, belonging to oneself, hard, solid" (MN 28.6/M I 185)—this is characteristic earth. (2) In the passage: "If he should dig the earth, or cause the earth to be dug" (SVibh Pācittiya 10/Vin IV 33)—this is composite earth. The twenty parts of the body beginning with head-hairs, etc., and the external elements such as iron and copper are also included in composite earth. For composite earth consists of earth together with its accompanying material dhammas, such as colour, etc.[22] (3) "Someone perceives the earth-kasiṇa" (DN 33.3.3/D III 268)—here the objectified earth is the earth-kasiṇa, also called the earth-sign *(nimittapaṭhavī).*[23] (4) "Earth as conventional designation": somebody who obtains jhāna with the earth-kasiṇa as basis, and is reborn in the world of the gods, gains the name "earth deity" after his means of arriving at such a state.

All these meanings of the word "earth" are relevant to the present context. For whatsoever instance among these four kinds of earth the worldling perceives as earth, he perceives (with the notion) "it is earth"; he perceives as a segment of earth *(paṭhavībhāgena)*; he perceives through a perversion of perception, seizing upon the conventional expression (and thinking) "it is earth" *(lokavohāraṃ gahetvā saññāvipallāsena sañjānāti).* Or, without releasing such a segment of earth, he perceives it as a being *(satta)* or as belonging to a being. Why does he perceive it in this way? This should not be asked, for the worldling is like a madman. He seizes upon anything he can in whatever way he can. Or else, the reason is that he has no regard for the ariyans, etc.; or, as the Exalted One will say later on, "because it has not been fully understood by him."

**Sub. Cy.** The base of conceiving is apprehended merely through hearsay, etc. Thus characteristic earth is included by mentioning "hard, solid," etc. But some raise the objection: "No conceiving takes place when the characteristic is seen, and the perception which seizes upon (the object) as a solid mass *(piṇḍagāhikā saññā)* and becomes the root for the assumption of views, does not recognize the characteristic. Therefore characteristic earth should not be included."[24] This is incorrect, for the penetration of the characteristic is not intended here; thus the commentator says: "seizing upon the conventional expression." And not all perception seizes upon the mass, nor does all become the root for the assumption of views. Therefore, conceiving also occurs in regard to the characteristic earth which appears through the body-door and elsewhere. Thus it was said that the base is "apprehended merely through hearsay, etc." Since the worldling, when he perceives any of these four kinds of earth, perceives it only as a portion of earth, and not as a portion of water, etc., it is said: "he perceives as a segment of earth." "Seizing upon the conventional expression": in this way the commentator shows that the perception of characteristic earth also occurs through the medium of the conventional expression.

*Objection:* If the conventional expression is applied, what is the fault? Don't ariyans also make use of the conventional expression, as when they say: "This, venerable sir, is the great earth," etc.?

*Reply:* It is not the mere employment of the expression that is intended here, but the wrong adherence which occurs through the conventional expression. Thus he says: "he perceives through a perversion of perception." This is the meaning: He perceives it as beautiful, etc.,[25] through a perverted perception springing from unwise reflection. By this, weak conceiving through craving, conceit, and views is shown.

If so, it may be asked, why is perception mentioned? Because it is evident. Just as, when a fire is smoldering and smoke is seen, although the fire still exists, we say "there is smoke" rather than "there is fire," because the smoke is more evident; in an analogous way, although conceiving is already exercising its function (in this perception), this function is not distinct. The function of perception alone is distinct, for perception is more evident. But this perception accords with the conceiving and works in conjunction with the latter; therefore he says: "he perceives through a perversion of perception." And when it is said that he perceives it thinking "it is earth," he means that, without releasing a segment of earth from among these four kinds, he perceives what is in its true nature devoid of self, etc., as endowed with a self, etc., like one perceiving a lump on the head as a piece of gold.

## "Having perceived earth as earth"

**Cy.** Having perceived earth thus with a perverted perception, the worldling afterwards conceives it, i.e., construes or discriminates it, through the strengthened proliferating tendencies of craving, conceit, and views, which are here called "conceivings" *(aparabhāge thāmapattehi taṇhāmānadiṭṭhipapañcehi idha maññanānāmena vuttehi maññati kappeti vikappeti).* This accords with the statement: "Concepts due to proliferation are grounded upon perception" *(saññānidānā hi papañcasaṅkhā,* Sn 874). He apprehends it in diverse ways contrary (to reality) *(nānappakārato aññathā gaṇhāti)*; hence it is said: "He conceives earth." To show that conceiving by which he conceives it by a gross method, the twenty parts of the body such as head-hairs, body-hairs, etc., may be mentioned as internal earth (MN 28.6/M I 185, Vibh §173/Vibh 82). The external earth may be understood through the passage in the *Vibhaṅga:* "What is the external earth element? Whatever is external, and is hard, solid, hardness, the state of being hard, exterior, not kammically acquired, such as: iron, copper, tin, lead, silver, pearl, gem, cat's-eye, shell, stone, coral, silver coin, gold, ruby, variegated precious stone, grass, wood, gravel, potsherd, earth, rock, mountain" (Vibh §173/Vibh 82). The earth-sign in the triad of internal objects may also be included.[26] This is the interpretation of the meaning.

**Sub. Cy.** *Papañcasaṅkhā = portions of papañca (papañcakoṭṭhāsa).* Because of these, beings are detained *(papañcanti)* in *saṃsāra*, i.e., delayed, thus these are "proliferating tendencies." "Conceiving" *(maññanā)*: because of these, people conceive, i.e., misconstrue *(parikappenti),* things as "This is mine," etc. Craving, conceit, and views are referred to here by two synonymous terms, "conceivings" and "proliferating tendencies."

"He apprehends it … contrary (to reality)": like the conceiving of views, the conceivings of craving and conceit also apprehend things contrary to reality—craving assuming the repulsive to be beautiful, conceit the inferior to be superior, etc. Just as applied thought and the other jhāna factors, despite their distinct specific natures, are nevertheless all jhāna factors in so far as they share the common nature of closely contemplating the object, in the same way, craving, conceit, and views—despite their distinct specific natures as yearning *(anugijjhana),* self-inflation *(uṇṇati),* and misapprehension *(parāmāsa),* respectively—are all forms of conceiving in so far as they occur in the common mode of misconstruing the object *(ārammaṇaparikappanākārena pavatti).* The "earth-sign" is the counterpart sign *(paṭibhāganimitta)* of the earth-kasiṇa.

### "He conceives (himself as) earth" (*paṭhaviṃ maññati*)

**Cy.** Through the three conceivings he conceives "I am earth," "earth is mine," "another is earth," "earth belongs to another."

**Sub. Cy.** The commentary shows the three conceivings in relation to one's own continuum and the continua of others in a condensed interpretation.[27] "I am earth": by this he shows the conceiving of views and the conceiving of conceit with an internal object, for this phrase implies adherence to a view of self *(attābhinivesa)* or I-making *(ahaṃkāra).* "Earth is mine"—this signifies the conceiving of craving and the conceiving of conceit; the latter is a possible interpretation because through conceit one considers oneself superior (equal or inferior) on account of some segment of earth which has come into one's possession. Conceiving may be analyzed in relation to the other two phrases in the same way.

One who obtains jhāna through the earth-kasiṇa may adhere to the object perceived in his meditation-vision as a self; or he may take that object as a sign of his superiority. Thus he conceives "I am earth" (through the conceivings of views and conceit, respectively). Apprehending this kasiṇa object as "*my* self," he conceives "earth is mine." On the other hand, if he adheres to this object doctrinally as another person or as a god, he conceives "another is earth"; and if he adheres to it as the self of another, he conceives "earth belongs to another."

**Cy.** Or, alternatively, he conceives internal earth through the conceiving of craving, through the conceiving of conceit, and through the conceiving of views. How? He arouses desire and lust for the head-hairs, etc.; he relishes *(assādeti)* them, delights in them, welcomes them, and remains holding to them. And so too for the body-hairs, nails, teeth, skin, or any other stimulating object. Thus he conceives internal earth through the conceiving of craving. Or he brings delight to bear upon them thus: "Let my head-hairs, etc., be thus in the future! Let my body-hairs be thus!," etc. Or resolving his mind on the acquisition of what he has not obtained, he thinks: "By this virtue or observance or austerity or holy life *(brahmacariya)*, may I have moist, soft, delicate blue-black hair," etc. Thus in this way he conceives internal earth through the conceiving of craving.

Again, on account of the beauty or ugliness of his own head-hairs, etc., he arouses conceit: "I am superior" or "I am equal" or "I am inferior." Thus he conceives internal earth through the conceiving of conceit.

He adheres to the head-hairs, etc., as a soul *(jīva),* according to the method that has come down: "The soul and the body are the same" (MN 63.2/M I 426)—thus he conceives internal earth through the conceiving of views. Or else, in direct contrast to the method given in the suttas (which involves contemplating): "The internal earth element and the external earth element are only the earth element; this is not mine" (MN 28.6/M I 185), he adheres to the earth element analyzed into the head-hairs, etc., as, "This is mine, this am I, this is my self." In this way too he conceives internal earth through the conceiving of views.

Thus he conceives internal earth through the three conceivings.

As the internal, so the external. How? He arouses desire and lust for iron, copper, etc.; he relishes them, delights in them, welcomes them, and remains holding to them. Thinking "iron is mine, copper is mine," etc., he takes possession of them (*mamāyati*), guards them, and keeps watch over them. Thus he conceives external earth through the conceiving of craving. Or he brings delight to bear upon them thus: "Let my iron, copper, etc., be thus in the future!" Or resolving his mind on the acquisition of what he has not obtained, he thinks: "By this virtue or observance or austerity or holy life, may I be one who possesses accessories made of iron, copper, etc." In this way too he conceives external earth through the conceiving of craving.

Again, on account of the beauty or ugliness of his own iron or copper possessions, etc., he arouses conceit: "I am superior" or "I am equal" or "I am inferior." Thus he conceives external earth through the conceiving of conceit.

Then, perceiving a soul in iron, he adheres to iron as a soul; the same method in regard to copper, etc. Thus he conceives external earth by the conceiving of views. Or else he interprets the earth-sign as a self according to the method given in the

Paṭisambhidāmagga: "Herein, someone considers the earth-kasiṇa as the self; thinking 'The earth-kasiṇa is I, I am the earth-kasiṇa,' he considers the earth-kasiṇa and the self as non-dual" (Paṭis 2.50/ Paṭis I 143). In this way too he conceives external earth though the conceiving of views.

Thus he conceives external earth through the three conceivings. In this way the statement "he conceives earth" is to be interpreted in terms of the three conceivings. The remainder we will discuss only in brief.

### "He conceives (himself) in earth" (*paṭhaviyā maññati*)

**Cy.** Here "in earth" is the locative case. Therefore he conceives "I am in earth"; he conceives "There is an obstruction *(kiñcana),* an impediment *(paḷibodha),* for me in earth"; he conceives "Another is in earth"; he conceives "There is an obstruction, an impediment, for another in earth." This is the meaning here.

**Sub. Cy.** Since "in earth" is a locative expression, the statement means that he construes the basis for conceiving (i.e., the earth element) as a receptacle *(ādhāra)* for his self, for the self of another, and for the accessories of both.

*Query:* Isn't it true that composite earth is a receptacle-support *(ādhāranissaya)* for the succession of dhammas, both those connected and unconnected with the faculties? And the others—characteristic earth, the earth-kasiṇa sign, and the earth deities—object-supports *(ārammaṇanissaya)* for the mental factors which take them as their objects? So there is nothing wrong here (i.e., when the worldling conceives earth as a receptacle).

*Reply:* No, because he *misconstrues (parikappanato)* the basis of conceiving as a support. For through the conceivings of views and conceit he takes earth as the support for "I," i.e., for a self, the referent of these conceivings. Thus he conceives "I am in earth." And through the conceiving of craving, he takes earth as the support for the self's accessories, the referent of this conceiving. Thus he conceives "There is an obstruction, an impediment, for me in earth."

**Cy.** Or, alternatively, this statement may be interpreted according to the following method: "How does one consider the self to be in material form? Here someone regards feeling, perception, the mental formations, and consciousness as the self, and thinks: 'This is my self; that self of mine (is embodied) in this material form.' Thus he regards the self as in material form" (Paṭis 2.80/ Paṭis I 145). In this way, assuming such things as feeling, etc., to be the self, he misconstrues some instance of earth, either internal or external, to be the locus *(okāsa)* for this self. Conceiving "This self of mine is in this earth," he conceives in earth. This is the way he conceives through views. The conceivings of craving and conceit should be understood as the affection *(sineha)* he arouses for this (supposed) self of his, and the conceit based upon it. When, in this same way, he conceives the self of another to be in earth, this is the conceiving of views. But the other types of conceiving are also recognized.

**Sub. Cy.** When he says "in material form," he includes the part (i.e., the earth element) by mentioning the whole (i.e., material form).[28] Since the whole can never be found without its parts, by mentioning the whole the part is also included.

"The other types of conceiving are also recognized": when one regards another as superior, etc., on account of his success, power, etc., taking his self to exist with earth as dependence-support *(sannissaya)*—this is the conceiving of conceit. And when one resolves one's mind upon these objects (with the same underlying assumption)—this is the conceiving of craving.

### "He conceives (himself apart) from earth" (*paṭhavito maññati*)

**Cy.** Here "from earth" is the ablative case. Therefore, "he conceives from earth" should be understood to mean that he conceives himself or another together with their accessories to originate *(uppatti)* or to emanate *(niggamana)* from earth with its aforesaid divisions, or he conceives the self to be other than the earth *(paṭhavito añño attā)*. This is his conceiving of views. The conceivings of craving and conceit can be understood as the affection and conceit he arouses in regard to the same base conceived by him with the conceiving of views. Others take the phrase "he conceives from earth" to mean that after developing meditation upon a limited earth-kasiṇa, he assumes the existence of an immeasurable self which is different from the kasiṇa object, and conceives "my self is external to earth."

**Sub. Cy.** "To originate or to emanate from earth": origination from earth can be interpreted by way of the doctrine of the primordial egg *(brahmaṇḍavāda)*: "Then there existed an egg made of gold. Brahmā himself originated in that."[29] Or it can be understood by way of the doctrine of atomism *(aṇukavāda),* which holds that the molecule *(dviaṇuka)* originates from the coupling of atoms. Emanation from earth can be interpreted by way of theism *(issaravāda)* with its doctrine of the creative play of God *(issarakuttato),* which maintains that all this world emerged from God.

"He conceives the self to be other than the earth": he takes the self to be water, etc.

In the first alternative (the self as originating or emanating from earth) the ablative has the characteristic of agency *(kārakalakkhaṇa)*; in the second (the self as other than earth) it has the characteristic of contrast *(upapadalakkhaṇa).*

### "He conceives 'earth is mine'" (*paṭhaviṃ me ti maññati*)

**Cy.** Here he lays claim to the entire great earth by way of craving; thus in this case only one conceiving, that of craving, is relevant. This interpretation applies to all instances of earth, internal and external, divided according to the aforesaid classification, thus: "Head-hairs are mine, body-hairs are mine, iron is mine, copper is mine."

**Sub. Cy.** Just as, when affection and conceit are aroused for a base conceived by views, the conceivings of craving and conceit arise, so we can understand that when one ranks oneself as superior, etc., on account of a base conceived by craving, or misconstrues that base as the property of a self and the self as its permanent master, then the conceivings of conceit and views arise.

"He delights in earth" (*paṭhaviṃ abhinandati*)

**Cy.** He delights in earth with its aforementioned classifications; he relishes it, clings to it, is what is meant.

If this meaning has already been shown by the statement "he conceives earth," why is this said ("he delights in earth")? This has not been explained by the ancients,[30] but this is my own opinion: as a display of elegance in teaching *(desanāvilāsa)* or in order to point out the danger *(ādīnava)*. For the Exalted One has fully penetrated that element of Dhamma *(dhammadhātu)* which, when fully penetrated, confers elegance in teaching through diverse and variegated methods. Therefore, after first showing the origination of defilements by way of conceiving, he now shows the same thing by way of delighting, as an example of his elegance in teaching. Or else: One who conceives earth, conceives in earth, conceives from earth, conceives "earth is mine," is not able to abandon the craving or views founded upon earth; therefore he also delights in earth. But he who delights in earth delights in suffering *(dukkha)*, and suffering is the danger. Thus he says this in order to point out the danger. For the Exalted One has said: "Bhikkhus, he who delights in the earth element delights in suffering. He who delights in suffering, I declare, is not released from suffering" (SN 14:35/S II 174).

**Sub. Cy.** "That element of Dhamma": the supreme enlightenment. This is called an element *(dhātu)* because it bears *(dhāreti)*, bears up *(upadhāreti)*, all knowable dhammas according to their specific nature; or because it bears up the entire succession of dhammas (in the continua) of the beings to be trained, preventing them from falling into the suffering of the planes of misery and the suffering of *saṃsāra*; and because it occurs in an unperverted mode. The supreme enlightenment is the path-knowledge (of the Buddha) founded upon his knowledge of omniscience, and his knowledge of omniscience founded upon his path-knowledge.

"Conceiving" is the misconstruing *(parikappanā)* of the object which occurs by way of desiring, self-promotion, and misapprehension *(abhikaṅkhanasampaggahaparāmasana)*.[31] The misconstruing is the adherence to the object as "I" and "mine." "Delighting," on the other hand, is that through which holding *(ajjhosāna)* occurs. This is the difference between conceiving *(maññanā)* and delighting *(abhinandanā).*

> "What is the reason? Because it has not been fully understood by him, I declare." *(apariññātaṃ tassā ti vadāmi)*

**Cy.** Having thus shown the (worldling's) conceiving and delight based upon earth, with these words the Master reveals the reason why the worldling conceives and delights in earth. This is the meaning: If it is asked, "For what reason does the worldling conceive earth? Why does he conceive and delight in earth?" the answer is: "because it has not been fully understood by him," i.e., because he has not fully understood the base, therefore (he does so). He who fully understands the earth understands it by the three types of full understanding: the full understanding of the known *(ñātapariññā),* the full understanding of scrutinization *(tīraṇapariññā),* and the full understanding of abandoning *(pahānapariññā).*

Therein, what is the full understanding of the known? He fully understands the earth element thus: "This is the internal earth element, this the external. This is its characteristic, this its function, manifestation, and proximate cause." This is full understanding of the known.

What is the full understanding by scrutinization? Having known it in this way, he scrutinizes the earth element in forty-two modes as impermanent, suffering, a sickness, etc.[32] This is full understanding by scrutinization.

What is the full understanding by abandoning? Having scrutinized it in this way, he abandons desire and lust for the earth element through the supreme path (*aggamagga*). This is full understanding by abandoning.

Or, alternatively, the defining of mentality-materiality *(nāmarūpavavatthāna)* is the full understanding of the known; from insight-comprehension of the groups *(kalāpasammasana)* as far as conformity knowledge *(anuloma)* is the full understanding by scrutinization; and the knowledge of the ariyan path is the full understanding by abandoning.

He who fully understands earth understands it by these three full understandings. But for the worldling there is no such full understanding. Therefore, due to his lack of full understanding, he conceives earth and delights in it. Hence the Exalted One said: "Herein, bhikkhus, an uninstructed worldling … conceives (himself as) earth … What is the reason? Because it has not been fully understood by him, I declare."

**Sub. Cy.** Therein, the "full understanding of the known" is the wisdom of full understanding by which one fully understands, delimits *(paricchindati),* the plane of insight *(vipassanābhūmi).* For this understands the dhammas of the three planes, delimiting them as internal and external and defining their characteristics, functions, etc.; thereby it makes it known, understood, evident, that "this is the plane of insight." Here it should be understood in terms of the earth element. The "full understanding of scrutinization" understands the five clinging aggregates in their true nature as impermanent, (suffering, and non-self,) by delimiting them through insight-comprehension and scrutinizing their modes of impermanence, etc., together with their accompaniments. The "supreme path" is the path of arahatship, for this abandons desire and lust without remainder; or it is the supramundane path (in general). Either is the full understanding of abandoning, which in the abstract sense is the wisdom which abandons (defilements) by eradicating them *(samucchedapahānakārī paññā).*

## 3. The Section on Water, etc.

**Cy.** "Water as water" *(āpaṃ āpato).* Here, water too is fourfold: characteristic, composite, objectified, and conventional designation. Among these, (1) characteristic water is explained thus: "What is the internal water element? That which is internal, belonging to oneself, water, liquidity, moisture, moistness, the internal coherence factor of matter, kammically acquired," etc. (Vibh §174/ Vibh 83; see too MN 28.11/M I 187 ). (2) "Taking up the water kasiṇa, he apprehends the sign in water"—this is composite water. The rest is the same as in the case of earth. But by way of interpretation, the internal water element is given with the twelve items beginning thus: "Bile, phlegm," etc. (see MN 28.11/M I 187). The external water element should be understood thus: "What is the external water element? That which is external, water, liquidity, moisture, moistness, the external coherence factor of matter, not kammically acquired, such as: the sap of roots, the sap of tree-trunks, the sap of bark, the juice of leaves, the juice of flowers, fruit juice, milk, curd, ghee, butter, oil, honey, molasses, and waters in the earth or atmosphere" (Vibh §174/Vibh 83). The water-sign in the triad of internal objects is also included.

"Fire as fire" *(tejaṃ tejato)*. In the section on fire too, the detailed account should be understood according to the aforementioned method. But by way of interpretation, the internal fire element is stated in terms of a fourfold division thus: "That by which one is warmed, by which one ages, by which one is heated, and by which whatever is eaten, drunk, chewed, and tasted gets fully digested" (MN 28.16/M I 188; Vibh §175/Vibh 83). The external fire element should be understood thus: "What is the external fire element? That which is external, fire, fiery, heat, hotness, warmth, warmness, external, not kammically acquired, such as: a log fire, a splint fire, a grass fire, a cow-dung fire, a husk fire, a rubbish fire, lightning (Indra's fire), the heat of a fire, the heat of the sun, the heat from an accumulation of logs, the heat from an accumulation of grass, grain, and wares" (Vibh §175/Vibh 83).

"Air as air" *(vāyaṃ vāyato)*. The same method as above also applies in this section on air, but by way of interpretation, the internal air element is stated thus: "Winds moving upwards, winds moving downwards, winds residing in the bowels, winds residing in the abdomen, winds moving along in all the limbs, sharp winds, cutting winds, rending winds, inhalation, exhalation" (MN 28.21/M I 188; Vibh §176/Vibh 84) The external air element should be understood thus: "What is external air element? That which is external, air, airy, the external distension of matter, not kammically acquired, such as: the easterly winds, the westerly winds, northerly winds, southerly winds, dusty winds, dustless winds, cold winds, hot winds, gentle winds, strong winds, black winds, high-altitude winds, wing winds, *supaṇṇa* winds, winds from a palm-leaf, winds from a fan" (Vibh §176/Vibh 84). The rest by the aforesaid method.

When one thing is mentioned, all
Things of like characteristic
Are mentioned too: this constitutes
The mode of conveying the characteristic.[33]

This is the mode of conveying the characteristic *(lakkhaṇa-hāra),* defined in the *Nettippakaraṇa.* By this principle, when the four primary elements are mentioned, derivative materiality *(upādā rūpa)* is implied along with them, since it shares the characteristic of material form. The primaries together with derivative materiality make up the aggregate of material form. Therefore, the assertion that the uninstructed worldling conceives earth, water, fire, and air signifies that he regards material form as the self. The assertion that he conceives in earth ... in air signifies that he regards the self to be in material form. The assertion that he conceives from earth ... from air, which implies the self to be other than material form, signifies that he regards the self to be possessed of material form or material form to be in the self. Thus these are the four conceivings of personality view *(sakkāyadiṭṭhimaññanā)* based upon materiality. One is the annihilationist view *(ucchedadiṭṭhi),* three are the eternalist view (*sassatadiṭṭhi)*; thus these reduce to only two views. This distinction should be understood.

**Sub. Cy.** By showing the conceiving of personality view, the conceivings of craving and conceit based on materiality are also shown. For these take the form of the affection and conceit he arouses for the base he conceives through the conceiving of views. Or else the conceiving of craving based on materiality is shown by the statements that he conceives the elements as "mine" and delights in them, with the conceiving of conceit following it in conformity.

## 4. The Section on Beings, etc.

### "He perceives beings as beings" (*bhūte bhūtato sañjānāti*)

**Cy.** Having explained the conceiving based on formations under the heading of material form, now, since the worldling arouses conceivings towards the beings who are discerned by reference to formations themselves,[34] the Exalted One sets out to expound these living beings, beginning with the above words.

Therein, the word "being" *(bhūta)* is found in the following senses: the five aggregates *(khandhapañcaka),* non-humans *(amanussa),* elements *(dhātu),* existing *(vijjamāna),* the cankerless one *(khīṇāsava),* living beings *(satta),* trees *(rukkha),* etc. In the passage: "Do you see, bhikkhus, that this has come into being *(bhūtam idaṃ)?*" (MN 38.9/M I 260), it is the five aggregates. "Whatever beings are here assembled" (Sn 222)—here it is non-humans. "The four primary elements *(mahābhūtā)* are the cause" (MN 109.9)—here it is the elements. "If a fact, an offence requiring expiation" (SVibh Pācittiya 8/Vin IV 25)—here, existing. "The being who swallows time" (J 245/Ja II 260)—here, the cankerless one. "All beings lay down the body in the world" (DN 16.6.10/D II 157)—here, living beings. "The destruction of plant life" *(bhūtagāma)* (DN 1.1.10/D I 5)—here, trees. In the present case the meaning of living beings applies. But not without a distinction; for here "beings" signifies only living beings below the heaven of the Four Great Kings *(cātumahārājikā).*[35]

Therein, "he perceives beings as beings"—the method (of interpretation) has been stated.[36] "He conceives beings, etc.": this and the following can be interpreted through the three conceivings. How? "He sees a householder or a householder's son supplied and furnished with the five strands of sense pleasure" (AN 7:47/A IV 55)—having apprehended beings in this way, he takes hold of the notion that "beings are beautiful" or "beings are happy" and becomes attached. Having seen them, having heard, smelled, tasted, touched, cognized them, he becomes attached: thus he conceives beings through the conceiving of craving. Or resolving his mind on the acquisition of what he has not obtained, he thinks: "Oh, that I may be reborn in the company of great wealthy khattiyas,"[37] etc. Thus too he conceives beings through the conceiving of craving. But depending on his excellence or deficiency in relation to other beings, he ranks himself as superior to others, or as inferior, or as equal. As it is said: "Herein, someone on account of birth … or on a certain ground previously ranked himself as equal to others; at a later time he ranks himself as superior and others as inferior. Such a kind of conceit is called arrogance *(mānātimāna)*" (Vibh § 880/ Vibh 355). Thus he conceives beings through the conceiving of conceit.

When he conceives beings thus: "Beings are permanent, stable, eternal, not subject to change," or "All living beings, all creatures, all beings, all souls are without power, without strength, without energy, evolving in the grip of fate, chance, or nature, experiencing pleasure and pain in the six classes" (DN 2.20/D I 53)—this is the conceiving of views.

In this way he conceives beings through the three conceivings.

How does he conceive (himself) "in beings" *(bhūtesu maññati)*? When he wishes for his own rebirth or attainment of happiness among such and such beings, he conceives in beings through the conceiving of craving. Or when he gives a gift, undertakes precepts, or observes the Uposatha,[38] wishing for rebirth among those beings (as a result of his merit), in this way too he conceives in beings through the conceiving of craving. When, having apprehended beings in terms of an aggregation *(samūhaggāhena),* he ranks some beings as superior, some as equal, some as inferior (in relation to himself), he conceives in beings through the conceiving of conceit. Thus too he conceives some beings as permanent and stable, some as impermanent and unstable, or he conceives "I too am a certain somebody among beings"—thus he conceives in beings through the conceiving of views.

"He conceives (himself apart) from beings" *(bhūtato maññati)*: he conceives (himself apart) from beings when he conceives himself or others together with their accessories to originate from some being; this is his conceiving of views. When he arouses affection and conceit for the base conceived through the conceiving of views, these are his conceivings of craving and conceit.

"He conceives 'beings are mine' " *(bhūte me ti maññati)*: here the conceiving of craving is alone relevant. This occurs when he lays claim to beings thus: "My sons, my daughters, my goats and sheep, my poultry and swine, my elephants, cattle, horses, and mares." "He delights in beings": the method has been stated (in the section on earth). "Because they have not been fully understood by him": the beings are not fully understood because he has not fully understood the formations by reference to which beings are discerned. The interpretation should be made by the method stated.

Having thus shown in brief the bases of conceiving by way of formations and living beings, now, with the words "gods as gods," the Exalted One sets out to show the same thing in detailed classification according to the division of planes. Therein, they revel *(dibbanti)* in the five strands of sense pleasure or in their own psychic powers, thus they are called gods *(devas)*; they play *(kīḷanti)* or they shine *(jotenti)* is the meaning. There are three kinds of "gods": gods by convention *(sammutideva),* gods by rebirth *(upapattideva),* and gods by purification *(visuddhideva).* Gods by convention are kings, queens, and princes. Gods by rebirth are the gods of the heaven of the Four Great Kings and the higher heavenly worlds. And gods by purification are arahats, cankerless ones. Here gods by rebirth are meant, and not without a distinction, for Māra and his retinue in the Paranimmitavasavatti heavenly world are excepted; only the remaining gods in the six sense sphere heavenly worlds are intended here as "gods." The entire explanation of the meaning should be understood in the way set forth in the section on beings.

"Pajāpati": here Pajāpati is Māra. Some say that this is a designation for the great kings, etc., who are overlords in the various groups of gods, but the Great Commentary[39] rejects this as incorrect, for these are already included under the category of gods. Māra alone is intended here by the word "Pajāpati," for he is the overlord *(adhipati)* of this generation *(pajāya)* made up of living beings. Where does he reside? In the Paranimmitavasavatti heavenly world.[40] Some say that the king of the Vasavattis exercises rule there, while Māra lives in one place wielding sovereignty over his own retinue like a rebel prince in a frontier corner of a kingdom. The retinue of Māra should be understood as included along with Māra.

Here is the interpretation: When he arouses desire after seeing or hearing that Pajāpati is beautiful, of long-life and abundant happiness, then he conceives him through the conceiving of craving. When he resolves his mind on the acquisition of what he has not obtained, thinking: "Oh, that I may be reborn in the company of Pajāpati!" in this way too he conceives Pajāpati through the conceiving of craving. When, after attaining the state of Pajāpati, he gives rise to the conceit: "I am the ruler of creatures, the overlord," he conceives Pajāpati through the conceiving of conceit. Thinking "Pajāpati is permanent and stable," or "Pajāpati will be annihilated and destroyed," or "Pajāpati is without power, without strength, without energy, evolving in the grip of fate, chance, or nature, experiencing pleasure and pain in the six classes," he conceives Pajāpati through the conceiving of views.

"In Pajāpati": here the conceiving of views is alone applicable. It arises when someone conceives: "Those dhammas which are found in Pajāpati are all permanent, stable, eternal, not subject to change." Or else he conceives: "There is no evil in Pajāpati, nor are any evil deeds found in him."

"From Pajāpati": here the three conceivings are relevant. How? Here someone conceives himself or another together with their accessories to originate or emanate from Pajāpati; this is his conceiving of views. When he arouses affection and conceit for the base conceived through the conceiving of views, these are his conceivings of craving and conceit. "Pajāpati is mine": here the conceiving of craving is alone relevant. This occurs when he lays claim to Pajāpati thus: "Pajāpati is my master, he is my lord." The rest by the method stated.

"Brahmā as Brahmā": he is magnified *(brūhita)* with distinguished qualities, thus he is Brahmā. Mahābrahmā is called "Brahmā"; so too is the Tathāgata, brahmins, mother and father, and what is supreme. In the passage: "Brahmā of one thousand, Brahmā of two thousand" (MN 120.13/M III 101), it is Mahābrahmā. " 'Brahmā', bhikkhus, this is a designation for the Tathāgata"—here it is the Tathāgata.

> Dispeller of darkness, enlightened one, universal eye,
> Gone to the world's end, transcending all existence,
> The cankerless, released from all suffering,
> The bringer of truth honoured by Brahmā (Sn 1133)

—here it is a brahmin. "Mother and father are called Brahmā, teachers of old" (It 106/It 110 )—here mother and father. "He sets in motion the wheel of Brahmā *(brahmacakka)*" (MN 12.9/M I 69)—

here (it is an adjective meaning) supreme. Here (in the text) it is the Brahmā who is first to be born and whose life-span lasts for the aeon that is intended. When he is mentioned, the ministers of Brahmā and the assembly of Brahmā should also be included.[41] The explanation of the meaning should be understood by the method stated in the section on Pajāpati.

"The gods of Streaming Radiance": a radiance *(ābhā)* streams forth *(sarati),* streams out *(visarati),* from their bodies like light from the flame of a torch, penetrating further and further and descending; thus they are gods of Streaming Radiance *(ābhassara).* By mentioning these, all (gods) occupying the plane of the second jhāna are included. All these occupy a single level: the gods of Limited Radiance *(parittābhā),* of Immeasurable Radiance *(appamāṇābhā),* of Streaming Radiance.

"The gods of Refulgent Glory" *(subhakiṇhā)*: they are covered with glory *(subhena okiṇṇā),* bestrewn with glory; their bodies are a single mass radiant and beautiful like a resplendent, blazing piece of gold placed in a golden casket. By mentioning these, all (gods) occupying the plane of the third jhāna are included. All these occupy a single level: the gods of Limited Glory *(parittasubhā),* of Immeasurable Glory *(appamāṇasubhā)*, of Refulgent Glory.

"The gods of Abundant Fruit" *(vehapphalā)*: these are Brahmās on the plane of the fourth jhāna. The interpretation of the meaning for these three sections is the same as the method stated in the section on beings.

He vanquishes, thus he is a Vanquisher *(abhibhū).* What does he vanquish? The four immaterial aggregates. This is a designation for the beings of the non-percipient realm. The non-percipient gods occupy one section of the same plane as the gods of Abundant Fruit, where they remain in the same posture in which they are reborn throughout their lives, all with similar material form resulting from the similarity of their productive kamma consciousness. All these are included here by the word "Vanquisher." Some say the Vanquisher is the Brahmā ruling a thousand (worlds) who is the overlord here and there, but this is incorrect, since this one is already included in the Brahmā section.

In the interpretation, when he arouses desire and lust after hearing that the Vanquisher is beautiful and long-lived, then he conceives the Vanquisher through the conceiving of craving. When he resolves his mind on the acquisition of what he has not obtained, thinking: "Oh, that I may be reborn in the company of the Vanquisher!" in this way too he conceives the Vanquisher through the conceiving of craving. Ranking himself as inferior and the Vanquisher as superior, he conceives him through the conceiving of conceit. Misapprehending the Vanquisher as permanent and stable, etc., he conceives him through the conceiving of views. The rest follows the method stated in the section on Pajāpati.

## 5. The Section on the Base of Infinite Space, etc.

**Cy.** Discussing the heavenly worlds in succession, the Exalted One shows the non-percipient realm and then skips over the pure abodes *(suddhāvāsā)* in order to discuss the base of infinite space *(ākāsānañcāyatana).* The reason he omits the pure abodes is because this is an explanation of the round of existence *(vaṭṭakathā),* and the pure abodes pertain to the ending of the round *(vivaṭṭa),* since they are inhabited exclusively by gods who are non-returners *(anāgāmī)* and arahats. Or the reason is that the life-span of these gods is only a few thousands of aeons, and they only exist during the time when a Buddha has appeared in the world. But Buddhas sometimes do not appear for an incalculable number of aeons, and during this time that plane (of the pure abodes) is empty. For the realm of the pure abodes belongs to the Buddhas like a campground to a king. For this reason they are not included in the (seven) stations of consciousness or the (nine) abodes of beings. But these conceivings occur at all times; therefore the Buddha only speaks of the planes which always exist.

The base of infinite space is the four aggregates based on this plane—the wholesome *(kusala)*, resultants *(vipāka),* and inoperatives *(kiriya)*[42]. But here only the aggregates of those reborn on that plane are meant, for this is a discussion delimiting the planes of existence. The same method in the case of the base of infinite consciousness, etc. The interpretation of the meaning in these four sections follows the method given in the section on the Vanquisher. But here the conceiving of conceit should be interpreted according to the method of the section on Pajāpati.

## 6. The Section on the Seen and Heard, etc.

**Cy.** Having thus shown the bases of conceiving in detail by classifying them into their distinct planes, etc., the Exalted One now shows all the dhammas of the three planes included in personality *(sakkāya)* which function as the bases of conceiving, by classifying them into a fourfold scheme as the seen, heard, sensed, and cognized.

Therein, the "seen" *(diṭṭha)* means what is seen by the fleshly eye and by the divine eye. This is a designation for the visible form base *(rūpāyatana)*. "He conceives (himself as) the seen": he conceives the seen with the three conceivings. How? (1) Seeing the visible form base in terms of the perception of beauty *(subhasaññā)* and the perception of pleasure *(sukhasaññā)*, he arouses desire and lust for it, relishes it, and delights in it. For this has been said by the Exalted One: "Beings become lustful, bhikkhus, over the form of a woman, entranced, infatuated, intoxicated, and fettered. Coming under the sway of the form of a woman, they sorrow for a long time" (AN 5:55/A III 68). Thus he conceives the seen with the conceiving of craving. Or he thinks: "May my body be thus in the future," and brings delight to bear upon it; or he gives alms yearning for the attainment of physical beauty, and so on in detail. In these ways too he conceives the seen with the conceiving of craving. (2) He arouses conceit on account of the excellence or deficiency of his own form in relation to another's, thinking: "I am superior to him," or "I am equal," or "I am inferior." Thus he conceives the seen with the conceiving of conceit. (3) He conceives the visible form base as permanent, stable, and eternal, or as a self or the property of a self, or as auspicious or inauspicious. Thus he conceives the seen with the conceiving of views. In this way he conceives the seen with the three conceivings.

How does he conceive himself "in the seen"? He conceives in the seen when he regards the self to be in visible form *(rūpasmiṃ attānam)*. Or he conceives in the seen when he thinks: "Lust, etc., are in visible form just as milk is in the mother's breast." This is his conceiving of views. The conceivings of craving and conceit are the affection and conceit he arouses in regard to the base conceived by the conceiving of views. Thus he conceives "in the seen." The remainder should be understood by the method stated in the section on earth.

**Sub. Cy.** "When he regards the self as in visible from": taking the immaterial dhammas such as feeling, etc., to be the self, or all dhammas apart from the visible form base, imagining the visible form base internally or externally as its container *(okāsa),* he conceives: "This self of mine is in this visible form base." Thus he conceives "in the seen."

**Cy.** "The heard" *(suta)*: what is heard by the fleshly ear and by the divine ear. This is a designation for the sound base *(saddāyatana).*

"The sensed" *(muta)*: that which is apprehended by sensing, i.e., by approach and contact. What is meant is that it is cognized through the mutual adherence of the sense faculty and objects. This is a designation for the bases of odour, flavour, and touch.[43]

"The cognized" *(viññāta)*: cognized with the mind. This is a designation for the remaining seven sense bases, or for the mental object *(dhammārammaṇa).* But here only that which is included in personality is applicable. In detail these sections should be understood by the method stated in the section on the seen.

## 7. The Section on Unity, etc.

**Cy.** Having thus shown all personality distributed into four classes, as the seen, etc., the Exalted One, by the words "unity" *(ekatta)* and "diversity" *(nānatta),* now shows the same as divided into two classes through a section on the attainer *(samāpannaka)* and on the non-attainer *(asamāpannaka).* By the word "unity" he shows the attainer, and by the word "diversity" the non-attainer.

**Sub. Cy.** "A section on the attainer": on the occasion of a jhāna pertaining to the fine-material sphere *(rūpāvacara)* or the immaterial sphere *(arūpāvacara).* Since the jhāna occurs in a single mode on a single object, it is called "unity." The occurrence of the resultant jhāna may also be included in the section on the attainer.

"A section on the non-attainer": on the occasion of the occurrence of sense sphere phenomena. For even in access concentration *(upacārajjhāna),* the mind has not completely attained to unity.

**Cy.** This is the word-meaning: unity = oneness *(ekabhāva),* diversity = manyness *(nānābhāva).* The four immaterial aggregates pertain to the case of the attainer, all five aggregates to the case of the non-attainer. The interpretation can be made by the method of the Dispensation (i.e., the canonical texts) thus: "He regards material form as the self," etc., or by the commentarial method given in the section on earth, having determined by investigation which is appropriate. But some say that unity indicates the method of unity *(ekattanaya)* and diversity the method of diversity *(nānattanaya).* Others say the adherence to the views "the self is immutable after death and percipient of unity/percipient of diversity" is meant. Neither of these is correct for they are not intended here.

Having thus shown all personality as twofold, now collecting it together he shows the same thing again as singlefold with the words "all as all" *(sabbaṃ sabbato).* This is the method of interpretation: Relishing all *(sabbaṃ assādento),* he conceives all through the conceiving of craving. Conceiving all as created by himself, thus: "These beings have been created by me," etc., he conceives all with the conceiving of conceit. "All is caused by past kamma," "All is created by God," "All is without cause, without condition," "All exists," "All does not exist," etc.—in these ways he conceives all through the conceiving of views.

How does he conceive himself "in all"? Here someone holds such a view: "My self is great" *(mahā me attā).* Imagining all the world as a dwelling, the container *(okāsa)* for the self, he conceives: "This self of mine is in all" *(so kho pana me ayaṃ attā sabbasmiṃ).* This is his conceiving of views. His conceivings of craving and conceit are the affection he arouses for this self and the conceit based upon it, respectively. The rest should be understood by the method stated in the section on earth.

**Sub. Cy.** "Relishing all": when there is no perception of the danger in all phenomena pertaining to the three planes, due to the absence of disenchantment *(nibbidā)* they are contemplated as satisfaction *(assāda)* and craving increases. For this has been said by the Exalted One: "For one who dwells contemplating satisfaction in things subject to the fetters, craving increases" (SN 12:53/S II 86).

"Conceiving all as created by himself": through conceit he conceives himself to be the creator, and ranks himself as superior, etc., by conceiving all to be created by him; for such a conceit only arises when he conceives himself to be the creator.

The "etc." after "all does not exist" indicates that fatalism *(niyativāda),* etc., should be included.

"My self is great": by this he shows the doctrine which regards all as the manifestation of the self *(attano vibhūtipavattivāda).*

"The rest should be understood by the method stated in the section on earth": the conceiving which occurs thus: "I am in all; an obstacle, an impediment, for me is in all; another is in all; an obstacle, an impediment, for another is in all."

He conceives himself apart "from all" when he holds the view that "All this world is made of spirit" *(sabbo'yaṃ loko purisamayo),* and conceives the origination or emanation of the self to proceed from the all consisting in spirit. The affection and conceit he arouses for the base conceived by the conceiving of views are his conceivings of craving and conceit, respectively.

Conceiving "All is my self, or my creator, or my master," he conceives "all is mine." Delighting in it with craving and views, "he delights in all." Thus the occurrence of the conceivings should be understood here.

**Cy.** Having shown all personality as singlefold, with the words "nibbāna as nibbāna" he shows the same as again singlefold by a different method. Here "nibbāna" should be understood as the five kinds of "supreme nibbāna here and now" (*paramadiṭṭhadhammanibbāna*) which have come down in the passage beginning: "When this self, furnished and supplied with the five strands of sense pleasure, revels in them, then it has attained to supreme nibbāna here and now" (DN 1.3.20/D I 36). Relishing this nibbāna, he conceives it with the conceiving of craving. The conceit he arouses because of this nibbāna when he thinks "I have attained nibbāna"—this is the way he conceives nibbāna through the conceiving of conceit. Holding that which is in reality not nibbāna to be nibbāna and to be permanent, etc., he conceives nibbāna through the conceiving of views.

Taking his self to be other than nibbāna, conceiving "This self of mine is in this nibbāna"—he conceives himself "in nibbāna." This is his conceiving of views. The affection he arouses for this self and the conceit based on it are his conceivings of craving and of conceit, respectively.

This is the method by which he conceives himself apart "from nibbāna": taking his self to be other than nibbāna, conceiving "This is nibbāna, this the self. This self of mine comes from nibbāna, it is other than nibbāna"—he conceives himself apart "from nibbāna." This is his conceiving of views. The affection he arouses for this self and the conceit based upon it are his conceivings of craving and of conceit, respectively. He conceives "nibbāna is mine" thus: "Oh, how blissful is my nibbāna!" The rest by the method stated.

**Sub. Cy.** Those who hold the doctrine of supreme nibbāna here and now conceive the five aggregates which have attained to the ultimate happiness *(ukkaṃsagatasukhasahitaṃ hi khandhapañcakaṃ)* to be nibbāna; but in reality, they remain only personality *(sakkāya).* The five kinds are the happiness of sense pleasures mentioned in the commentary, and the happiness of the four fine-material sphere jhānas.

**Cy.** Here is the summing up verse:

Because he does not understand
The person *(sakkāya)* as it really is
The worldling only generates
Conceivings in the person-group *(sakkāya).*

Though in truth foul and perishable,
painful, void of an inner lord *(aparināyaka),*
The fool takes it in the opposite way,
Grasps hold of it through his conceivings.

He contemplates the person-group
As beautiful and pleasurable,
Plunging in through conceivings of craving
Like a moth into a candle flame.

Standing on ideas of permanence,
Extolling himself for his excellence,
Like filth being poured into filth
Conceivings of conceit arise.

Like a madman his image in a glass,
The fool takes the self to be real,
And so too property of this self—
These are his conceivings in terms of views.

This that we have called "conceiving"
Is the very subtle bondage of Māra,
Flexible and difficult to break,
By this the worldling is held in thrall.

Though struggling and striving with all his might,
He does not escape the person-group,
But circles on like a leash-bound dog
Tied to a firmly planted post.

This worldling attached to the person-group
Is constantly slain with vehement force
By the pains of birth, disease, and age,
By all the sufferings of the round.

Therefore I say to you, good sir,
Discern the person with sharp insight
As bound to pain, an impure mass,
Subject to break up, void of self.

The sage perceiving as it is
This, the true nature of our being,
Abandons all conceiving's modes
And from all suffering finds release.

The discussion of the first method, the twenty-four sections by way of the worldling, is completed.

## 8. The Section on the Learner

**Cy.** So far the Exalted One has shown the cognitive process *(pavatti)* of the worldling in regard to the bases such as earth, etc., which process becomes the root of all the dhammas included in personality. Now, with the words "A bhikkhu who is a learner," he undertakes to show the cognitive process of the learner *(sekha)*[44] as it occurs in regard to these same bases.

In what sense is the learner called by this name? He is a learner because he has obtained the qualities that make him a learner. For this is said: "To what extent, Lord, is one a learner?" "Here, bhikkhus, a bhikkhu is endowed with a learner's right view ... a learner's right concentration. To this extent a bhikkhu is a learner" (SN 45:13/S V 14). Moreover, "he learns *(sikkhati),* therefore he is a learner." For this is said: "He learns, bhikkhu, thus he is called a learner. And what does he learn? He learns the higher virtue, the higher consciousness, and the higher wisdom. He learns, bhikkhu, thus he is called a learner" (AN 3:84/A I 231).

The noble-minded worldling *(kalyāṇaputhujjana)* who fulfils the practice in conformity (with the supramundane path, *anulomapaṭipadā),* who is endowed with virtue, restrained over the doors of the senses, moderate in eating, who applies himself to wakefulness, and is devoted to the development of the constituents of enlightenment in the first and last watches of the night, thinking: "Today or tomorrow I will achieve one of the fruits of recluseship"—he too is called a learner because he learns. But in this place only the learner who has attained to penetration is meant,[45] not even the noble-minded worldling.

"Who has not attained his heart's ideal" *(appattamānaso)*: the word *mānasa* has the meanings of lust *(rāga),* mind *(citta),* and arahatship. In the passage "The heart is a snare that wanders about in mid-air" (SN 4:15/S I 111), it means lust. "Mind, mentality, mentation *(mānasa)*"—here, mind. "A learner who has not attained his heart's ideal"—here, arahatship. In the present case too arahatship is intended. Thus the meaning is "who has not attained arahatship." "Supreme" *(anuttara)*: the best, the unequalled. "Security from bondage" *(yogakkhema)*: security from the four bonds.[46] Arahatship itself is intended. "Yearning" *(patthayamāno)*: there are two yearnings, the yearning of craving *(taṇhāpatthanā)* and the yearning of desire *(chandapatthanā)*. Here desire to do, the wholesome yearning of desire is intended. The phrase means that he desires to attain security from bondage, desires to achieve it; he slants, slopes, and inclines to it as his goal.

### "He directly knows earth as earth" (*paṭhaviṃ paṭhavito abhijānāti*)

**Cy.** He directly knows earth in its nature as earth *(paṭhavī-bhāvena)*, unlike the worldling who perceives it with a completely perverted perception. Further, he knows it with distinguished knowledge *(abhivisiṭṭhena ñāṇena)*. What is meant is that, resolving upon the earth in accordance with its real nature as earth, he knows it as impermanent, suffering, and non-self.

**Sub. Cy.** "With distinguished knowledge": without falling short of the true nature of dhammas and without overshooting the mark, as confused comprehension and wrong understanding do, he knows it with distinguished knowledge which directly confronts the true nature of dhammas without falling away from it. The meaning is: with the full understanding through scrutinization based on the full understanding of the known, and with one section *(ekadesa)* of the full understanding of abandoning.[47]

### "Let him not conceive (himself as) earth" (*paṭhaviṃ mā maññī*)[48]

**Cy.** He cannot be described either as one who conceives or as one who does not conceive. What is the purport here? Because he has not abandoned any of the conceivings, the worldling is described as one who conceives. The arahat, who has abandoned them all, is described as one who does not conceive. The learner has abandoned the conceiving of views, and has diminished the others. Therefore he cannot be described as one who conceives, like the worldling, nor can he be described as one who does not conceive, like the arahat.

**Sub. Cy.** *Mā maññī: mā* = he conceives by way of the unabandoned forms of conceiving; *amaññī* = he does not conceive by way of the abandoned forms of conceiving. Combined, the two yield *mā maññī.*

Or else *mā maññī* is a command prohibiting an optional action, like "Do not injure, do not hurt," etc. The meaning is: he should not conceive *(na maññeyya).* The learner cannot be described as "one who conceives" like the worldling who has not abandoned any of the conceivings, nor as "one who does not conceive" like the arahat who has abandoned them all. For him part of the conceivings are abandoned, part unabandoned. And though the conceivings that are unabandoned have been greatly diminished by him, he still should not conceive through those, much less through the others, due to the absence of a more distinct conceiving. This absence of conceiving *(amaññanā)* is for the purpose of fully understanding the base; it is not an absence of conceiving achieved through the full understanding of the base, as is the case with the arahat. Since it is possible for him to fully understand that which should be fully understood, conceivings do not arise for him in the way they do for the worldling, who is destitute (of that capacity).

### "Because it should be fully understood by him" (*pariññeyyaṃ tassa*)

**Cy.** The base of conceiving should be fully understood by the learner through the three full understandings, for he has entered the course of rightness *(okkantaniyāmattā)*[49] and is bound for enlightenment. Unlike the worldling he is not wholly lacking in full understanding, and unlike the arahat he has not completed full understanding.

## 9. The Section on the Cankerless One

**Cy.** Having thus shown the cognitive process of the learner in regard to the bases such as earth, etc., with the words "A bhikkhu who is an arahat," the Exalted One next undertakes to show the cognitive process of the cankerless one *(khīṇāsava).*

Therein, *arahat* = one who is remote from the defilements *(ārakakilesa),* far from the defilements. The meaning is: one who has abandoned the defilements. As the Exalted One says: "And how bhikkhus, is a bhikkhu an arahat? He is remote from evil, unwholesome states, from states which are defiling, leading to renewed existence, disturbing, bringing painful results, conducing to future birth, ageing and death. Thus, bhikkhus, a bhikkhu is an arahat" (MN 39.29/M I 280).

"A cankerless one": the four cankers *(āsava)* are the canker of sensual desire, the canker of desire for existence, the canker of wrong views, and the canker of ignorance. For the arahat these four cankers are destroyed, abandoned, eradicated, silenced, consumed by the fire of knowledge so that they can no more arise again; therefore he is called a cankerless one.

"Lived the holy life" *(vusitavā)*: he has lived in co-residence with his teacher, dwelt in the ariyan path, and abided in the ten ariyan abidings. He has lived the life, completed the course; thus he is one "who has lived the holy life."

"Done what had to be done" *(katakaraṇīyo)*: in comparison to the noble-minded worldling, the seven learners are doing what has to be done by the four paths. For the cankerless one all that should be done has been done and completed. There is nothing further for him to do to achieve the destruction of suffering; thus he has "done what had to be done." For this is said:

> For such a bhikkhu perfectly released,
> Who dwells with ever tranquil mind,
> There is no repetition of what he has done,
> Nor does anything remain that he must do. (Th 642)

"Laid down the burden" *(ohitabhāro)*: there are three burdens—the burden of the aggregates, the burden of the defilements, and the burden of kamma-formations. For the arahat these three burdens have been laid down, thrown down, deposited, cast down; therefore he is called one who has "laid down the burden."

"Attained his own goal" *(anuppattasadattho)*: by "own goal" arahatship is meant. For that is one's own goal, one's personal goal, in the sense that it is connected with oneself, that it can never be abandoned by oneself, and that it is one's supreme goal.

"Eliminated the fetters of existence" *(parikkhīṇabhava-saṃyojano)*: the ten fetters are the fetters of sensual lust, aversion, conceit, views, doubt, clinging to rules and rituals, lust for existence, jealousy, stinginess, and ignorance. These are called "fetters of existence" because they fetter *(saṃyojenti),* connect, beings to the states of existence, or because they fetter one existence to the next. These fetters of existence are eliminated by the arahat, abandoned, consumed by the fire of knowledge; therefore he is called one who has "eliminated the fetters of existence."

"Emancipated through final knowledge" *(sammadaññā vimutto)*: what is meant by "final knowledge"? He has known, scrutinized, investigated, clarified, and illuminated with knowledge perfectly, as it really is, the aggregates' meaning of aggregates, the bases' meaning of bases, the elements' meaning of elements, suffering's meaning of oppressing, the origin's meaning of source, cessation's meaning of peace, the path's meaning of seeing, or the division beginning thus: "All formations are impermanent," etc. "Emancipated": there are two emancipations, emancipation of mind *(cittassa vimutti)* and nibbāna. Since his mind is emancipated from all defilements, the arahat is emancipated by the emancipation of mind. And since he is resolved upon nibbāna *(nibbānaṃ adhimuttattā)* he is also emancipated in nibbāna. Therefore he is called "emancipated by final knowledge."

## "Because it has been fully understood by him" (*pariññātaṃ tassa*)

**Cy.** What is meant is that the arahat has fully understood the bases of conceiving through the three kinds of full understanding. Therefore he neither conceives the base nor does he conceive the conceiving. The remainder by the method stated.

At the end of the nibbāna section, three additional sections are stated in terms of the destruction of lust, hate, and delusion. Each should be applied to each of the sections dealing with the bases, beginning with earth, just as the statement on full understanding should be applied to all terms. Only one condensed statement is given since the meaning is the same in all cases.

### "Because he is devoid of lust through the destruction of lust" (*khayā rāgassa vītarāgattā*)

**Cy.** Those outside (the Buddha's Dispensation) who are devoid of lust for sensual pleasures are not "devoid of lust through the destruction of lust."[50] The arahat alone is. Therefore it is said: "Because he is devoid of lust through the destruction of lust." This method should also be applied to the cases of hate and delusion. Just as, when it is said "because it has been fully understood by him," the meaning is that because it has been fully understood he conceives neither the base nor the conceiving, so here too because he is devoid of lust he conceives neither the base nor the conceiving.

And here the section on full understanding is stated for the purpose of showing the fulfilment of the development of the path *(maggabhāvanāpāripūrī),* the others for the purpose of showing the fulfilment of the realization of the fruit *(phalasacchikiriyāpāripūrī).* Or else, the arahat does not conceive for two reasons: because he has fully understood the base and because he has eradicated the unwholesome roots. Therefore the section on full understanding shows his full understanding of the base, the others his eradication of the unwholesome roots.

In the three latter sections, the following distinction should be understood: Having seen the danger in lust, he dwelt in the contemplation of suffering, became emancipated through the deliverance of the wishless *(appaṇihitavimokkha),* and is devoid of lust through the destruction of lust. Having seen the danger in hate, he dwelt in the contemplation of impermanence, became emancipated through the deliverance of the signless *(animittavimokkha),* and is devoid of hate through the destruction of hate. Having seen the danger in delusion, he dwelt in the contemplation of non-self, became emancipated through the deliverance of emptiness *(suññatāvimokkha),* and is devoid of delusion through the destruction of delusion.

If such is the case, since no one becomes emancipated through three deliverances, shouldn't two sections be omitted? No. Why? Because there is no specification. For it was said "a bhikkhu who is an arahat" without specification. It was not said that he is emancipated by the wishless deliverance or by either of the other two; therefore all that is appropriate for an arahat should be mentioned.

Or else, without distinction, whoever is an arahat, by fully understanding the suffering in change *(vipariṇāmadukkha),* becomes devoid of lust through the destruction of lust; by fully understanding the suffering in painful feeling *(dukkhadukkha),* becomes devoid of hate through the destruction of hate; and by fully understanding the suffering in formations *(saṅkhāradukkha),* becomes devoid of delusion through the destruction of delusion. Or by fully understanding a desirable object *(iṭṭhārammaṇa),* he becomes devoid of lust through the destruction of lust; by fully understanding an undesirable object *(aniṭṭhārammaṇa),* he becomes devoid of hate through the destruction of hate; and by fully understanding a neutral object *(majjhattārammaṇa),* he becomes devoid of delusion through the destruction of delusion. Or by eradicating the latent tendency to lust for pleasant feeling, he becomes devoid of lust through the destruction of lust; and by eradicating the latent tendencies to aversion and delusion for painful and neutral feelings, respectively, he becomes devoid of hate and devoid of delusion. Therefore, showing these distinctions, the Exalted One says "devoid of lust, devoid of hate, devoid of delusion."

## 10. The Section on the Tathāgata

**Cy.** Having thus shown the cognitive process of the cankerless one in regard to the bases such as earth, etc., with the words "The Tathāgata, bhikkhus," the Exalted One next undertakes to show his own cognitive process.

Therein, "the Tathāgata": the Exalted One is called the Tathāgata for eight reasons: (1) because he has "thus come" *(tathā āgata)*; (2) because he has "thus gone" *(tathā gata)*; (3) because he has arrived at the real characteristic *(tathalakkhaṇaṃ āgata)*; (4) because he has awakened to real phenomena in accordance with actuality *(tathadhamme yāthāvato abhisambuddha)*; (5) because he is a seer of the real *(tathadassitāya)*; (6) because he is a speaker of the real *(tathāvāditāya)*; (7) because he acts in accordance with his teaching *(tathākāritāya)*; and (8) in the sense of surpassing *(abhibhavanaṭṭhena)*.[51]

He is an "arahat" for the following reasons: (1) because he is remote from the defilements *(āraka)*; (2) because his enemies *(ari)* and (3) the spokes have been destroyed *(hata)*; (4) because he is worthy *(araha)* to receive the requisites, etc.; and (5) because of absence of secret *(rahābhāva)* evil-doing. And he is a perfectly enlightened Buddha *(sammāsambuddha)* because he is perfectly *(sammā)* and by himself *(sāmaṃ)* enlightened *(buddha)* to all things. This is a summary; these two terms are elucidated in detail in the *Visuddhimagga,* in the explanation of the Recollection of the Buddha.[52]

"Because it has been fully understood to the end by the Tathāgata" (*pariññātantaṃ tathāgatassa*)

**Cy.** Here, the base of conceiving has been fully understood by the Tathāgata. It has been "fully understood to the end," fully understood to the conclusion, fully understood to the limit, fully understood without any remainder, is meant. For although there is no distinction between Buddhas and disciples in regard to the abandoning of defilements by the four paths, there is a distinction in regard to their range of full understanding. For disciples can attain nibbāna after insight-comprehension of only one segment of the four elements. But for the Buddhas there isn't even the slightest thing in the formations which has not been seen, weighed, scrutinized, and realized with knowledge.

"Because he has understood that delight is the root of suffering *(nandī dukkhassa mūlaṃ),* and that with existence (as condition) there is birth, and that for what has come to be there is ageing and death."

**Cy.** "Delight" is prior craving *(purimataṇhā),* "suffering" is the five aggregates *(pañcakkhandhā),* "root" is the beginning *(ādi).* "Having understood": he has known that the delight (occurring) in the previous existence is the root of the present suffering. "Existence" = kamma-existence. "Birth" = the resultant aggregates. Since those are born they are called "birth," or this teaching (is stated) under the heading of birth. This is the meaning: he has known that with kamma-existence (as condition) rebirth-existence occurs. "What has come to be" *(bhūta)* = a living being *(satta).* This is meant: he has known that ageing and death come upon the aggregates of the living being that has come to be through rebirth-existence.

To this extent, showing the cause for the absence of conceivings in him to be his penetration of dependent origination when he attained omniscience after comprehending the formations with insight while sitting in the invincible posture at the foot of the Bodhi tree, he shows dependent origination with its four sections *(catusaṅkhepa),* three links *(tisandhi),* three periods of time *(tiyaddha)* and twenty modes *(vīsat'ākāra).*[53]

How is all this shown? Here, delight is one section. Suffering is given as a second, existence is a third, and birth, ageing, and death are the fourth. Thus the four sections should be understood.[54] Between craving (= delight) and suffering there is one link, between suffering and existence a second, and between existence and birth a third. Thus, just as there are three links between the four fingers, there are also three links between the four groups. Delight belongs to the past period of time; birth, ageing, and death to the future; and suffering and existence to the present. Thus the three periods of time should be understood.

In the past there were five modes, of which craving alone has come down under the name "delight." But though they are not mentioned in the text, ignorance, formations, clinging, and existence are included along with craving, since they all share the characteristic of being conditions. The phrase "birth, ageing, and death" indicates the aggregates which are subject to birth, ageing, and death, and thus future consciousness, mentality-materiality, the sixfold base, contact, and feeling are implied.[55] These twenty modes have the characteristics described as follows: "In the previous kamma-existence, ignorance with its characteristic of delusion, formations of accumulating, craving of attachment, clinging of involvement, and existence of volition—these five states in the previous kamma-existence are conditions for rebirth-linking in this existence. Here, consciousness with its characteristic of rebirth-linking, mentality-materiality of descending, the bases of sensitivity, contact of touching, and feeling of being felt—these five states in the rebirth-existence in this life are conditioned by previously done kamma. With the maturation of the sense bases here, ignorance with its characteristic of delusion, formations of accumulating, craving of attachment, clinging of involvement, and existence of volition—these five states in the present kamma-existence are conditions for future rebirth-linking. In the future, consciousness with its characteristic of rebirth-linking, mentality-materiality of descending, the bases of sensitivity, contact of touching, and feeling of being felt—these five states in future rebirth-existence are conditioned by kamma done here."[56]

Thus by the statement: "He has understood that delight is the root of suffering, and that with existence (as condition) there is birth, and that for what has come to be there is ageing and death," this entire dependent origination with its four sections, three links, three periods of time, and twenty modes, is shown.

Next the Exalted One says:

> "Therefore, bhikkhus, through the complete destruction, fading away, cessation, abandoning, and relinquishing of all cravings, the Tathāgata has awakened to the supreme perfect enlightenment, I declare." (*tasmātiha bhikkhave tathāgato sabbaso taṇhānaṃ khayā virāgā nirodhā cāgā paṭinissaggā anuttaraṃ sammāsambodhiṃ abhisambuddho ti vadāmi*)

**Cy.** Here, "all cravings" is the same as delight. "Destruction" *(khaya)* is the ultimate destruction by the supramundane path. The following words are synonyms for destruction. For those cravings that are destroyed have also faded away, ceased, been abandoned, and been relinquished. Or else, "destruction" can be interpreted as the common function of the four paths, "fading away" *(virāga)* as the first path, "cessation" *(nirodha)* as the second, "abandoning" *(cāga)* as the third, and "relinquishing" *(paṭinissagga)* as the fourth.[57] Or else: through the "destruction" of those cravings by which he might perceive earth as earth; through the "fading away" of those by which he might conceive earth; through the "cessation" of those by which he might conceive in earth; through the "abandoning" of those by which he might conceive from earth; and through the "relinquishing" of those by which he might conceive "earth is mine." Or else: through the "destruction" of those by which he might conceive earth, and so forth until, through the "relinquishing" of those through which he might delight in earth. These interpretations are all possible; there is nothing to exclude them.

"Supreme perfect enlightenment" *(anuttara sammāsambodhi)*: the perfect enlightenment and self-enlightenment *(sammā sāmañca bodhi)* which is unsurpassed, the best of all. The word *bodhi* is used in the texts to signify a tree, the path, the knowledge of omniscience *(sabbaññutañāṇa),* and nibbāna. In the passages: "first enlightened at the foot of the Bodhi tree" and "between Bodhi and Gayā" (Mv I.1.1 & I.6.7/Vin I 1 & 8), it is the tree that is called *bodhi.*[58] In the passage: "The knowledge of the four paths is called *bodhi*" (Nidd II 57), it is the path.[59] In the passage: "He of the most excellent profound wisdom attained *bodhi*" (DN 30.1.27/D III 159), it is the knowledge of omniscience. In the following it is nibbāna: "Having attained to *bodhi,* the deathless, the unconditioned" *(untraced).* Here the Exalted One's knowledge of the path of arahatship is intended; others say the knowledge of omniscience as well.

Is the path of arahatship attained by disciples the supreme enlightenment or not? It is not. Why? Because it does not yield all the noble qualities *(guṇa).* For some disciples, the path of arahatship yields only the fruit of arahatship; for some the threefold knowledge; for some the six direct knowledges *(abhiññā)*; for some the four discriminations *(paṭisambhidā)*; for some the knowledge of the perfections *(pāramī)* of disciples. For paccekabuddhas it yields only the knowledge of a paccekabuddha's enlightenment. But for Buddhas it yields the endowment with all noble qualities, just as the coronation of a king confers sovereignty over all the nation. Therefore any other degree of enlightenment is not the supreme enlightenment.

"Awakened to" *(abhisambuddho)*: directly known, penetrated, attained, achieved. "I declare" *(iti vadāmi)*: I explain, teach, proclaim, establish, reveal, analyze, make manifest. Therein, this is the interpretation: "The Tathāgata, bhikkhus, does not conceive (himself as) earth ... does not delight in earth. What is the reason? Because he has understood that delight is the root of suffering, and that with existence (as condition) there is birth, and that for what has come to be there is ageing and death; what is meant is that he has understood, penetrated, this dependent origination. And what is more: since he has understood dependent origination thus, the craving called 'delight' has been abandoned in all its aspects by the Tathāgata. Through the complete destruction of all cravings, the Tathāgata has awakened to the supreme perfect enlightenment; therefore he does not conceive (himself as) earth ... does not delight in earth, I declare." This is meant: "By reason of his awakening he does not conceive and does not delight, I declare."

Or else: "Since cravings have gone to complete destruction through his understanding of dependent origination by the method, 'Delight is the root of suffering,' therefore, bhikkhus, through the complete destruction of all cravings, the Tathāgata has awakened to the supreme perfect enlightenment, I declare. By reason of his awakening, he does not conceive earth ... does not delight in earth."

## 11. Conclusion

"Thus spoke the Exalted One": the Exalted One spoke this entire sutta, from the end of the introduction to the words "awakened to the supreme perfect enlightenment, I declare," showing his supremely deep knowledge of omniscience which does not yield a foothold to the wisdom of others. The text comprises two recitation sections and eight major expository sections—one on the worldling, one on the learner, four on the arahat, and two on the Tathāgata. Each major section, in turn, contains twenty-four minor sections, from earth down to nibbāna.

But though this sutta, endowed with variegated methods and elegance of teaching, was spoken by the Exalted One with a Brahma-like voice sweet as the song of the cuckoo, pleasing to the ear, consecrating the hearts of the wise with the ambrosia of the deathless, "those bhikkhus did *not* delight in the word of the Exalted One." Why not? Because they didn't understand it. Since they didn't understand the meaning of the sutta, they didn't rejoice in it. For though endowed with variegated methods and elegance of teaching, at the time this sutta was for them like delicious food placed before a man with his mouth bound by a thick, broad cloth.

But didn't the Exalted One fulfil the perfections for four immeasurables plus 100,000 aeons and attain omniscience all for the purpose of teaching the Dhamma to others in a way they could understand? If so, why didn't they understand it in the way he taught it? The reason has been given in the section explaining the grounds for the delivery of this sutta: "He undertook this teaching for the purpose of shattering their conceit." Therefore this need not be repeated here. Having heard this sutta taught for the purpose of shattering their conceit, those bhikkhus thought: "The theorist, he says, perceives earth. The learner, the arahat, and the Tathāgata directly know it. What is this? How is this? Previously we could quickly understand whatever the Exalted One said. But now we cannot make head or tail out of this 'exposition of the root'. Oh, the Buddhas are immeasurable and unfathomable!" Thus they became humble, like snakes with drawn fangs, and went respectfully to attend upon the Buddha and listen to the Dhamma.

On that occasion a number of bhikkhus, sitting together in the Dhamma hall, started the following conversation:—"Oh, the spiritual power of the Buddhas! Those brahmin-monks were so puffed up with conceit, but the Master's teaching on the exposition of the root made them humble." This was the talk going on among these bhikkhus. Then the Exalted One came out from his Fragrant Cottage, went to the Dhamma hall displaying a wonder appropriate for the occasion, sat down in the special seat reserved for him, and said to the bhikkhus: "What kind of conversation were you having just now, bhikkhus?" They reported the matter to the Master. The Master said: "It is not only now, bhikkhus, but in the past as well that I humbled these men while they were going about with their heads swollen with conceit." Then the Exalted One related the following story of the past, a parallel to the present incident.

"Once upon a time, bhikkhus, a certain famous brahmin was living in Benares. He was master of the three Vedas with their vocabularies, liturgy, phonology and etymology, and the histories as a fifth; skilled in philology and grammar, he was fully versed in natural philosophy and in the marks of a Great Man.[60] He taught mantras to five hundred brahmin youths. Those youths, being clever, learned much quickly, bore it well in mind, and did not forget what they learned. The brahmin too did not have the closed fist of some teachers, but taught them every branch of knowledge as though pouring water into a jar, telling them: 'This branch of knowledge leads to so much welfare in this life and in the next.' In time those brahmin youths aroused the conceit: 'Whatever our teacher knows, that we know. We too can now be teachers.' From then on those youths became disrespectful towards their teacher and neglectful of their duties. The teacher, aware of the situation, thought: 'I will cut down their conceit.' One day, when they came to attend on him, after they had done homage and took their seats, he said: 'Dears, I will give you a riddle. Solve it if you can.' 'Give it, teacher, give it', they eagerly replied, so intoxicated were they with the pride of their learning. The teacher said:[61]

> 'Time swallows all beings that live
> Together with itself as well,
> But the being that swallows up this time—
> He consumes the consumer of beings.'

'Answer this riddle, dears.'

"But though they pondered it over and over, they couldn't figure it out, but could only remain silent. The teacher dismissed them: 'Enough for today, dears. Go, by tomorrow you should be able to answer it.'

"But even though ten and twenty of them tried to solve it together, still they couldn't make head or tail out of the riddle. The next day they went to the teacher and reported: 'We can't understand the meaning of this riddle.' The teacher, in order to cut down their conceit, recited this stanza:

> 'Many downy heads were held high with conceit,
> But some clever man has bound them by their necks.'

"Hearing this, those youths became silent, shame-faced, shoulders slumped, downcast, scratching the ground with their fingers.

Then the teacher, seeing that they were ashamed, said: 'Learn, dears, the solution to this riddle.' Then he explained:

"'Time' is the earlier part of the day and the later part of the day. 'Beings' are living beings. Time does not eat the skin and flesh of beings, but swallows and devours them by depriving them of life, beauty, and strength, by crushing their youth, and by destroying their health. 'Together with itself': thus devouring them, it does not omit anything but devours all. Not only does it devour all beings, but it also devours itself. For the earlier part of the day does not remain when the later part arrives, and the later part of the day does not remain when the next day arrives. 'The being who swallows up this time'—this is the arahat, the cankerless one. For he is called one who 'swallows up time' because he has 'eaten up' time by barring out the time of future rebirth. 'He consumes the consumer of beings': it is craving which consumes beings in the planes of misery. This the arahat has burnt up with the fire of knowledge and reduced to ashes. Thus he is said to 'consume the consumer of beings.'

"Through this explanation of their teacher those youths perceived the meaning of the riddle as clearly as the smooth and rough parts of a road illuminated at night by the light of a thousand lamps. They all vowed: 'As long as life lasts we will live under our teacher. Great, indeed, are these teachers! We were so puffed up with conceit on account of learning that we did not even know the meaning of a four-line stanza.' Humbled, from then on they performed their proper duties towards their teacher as they did in the past, and in the next life were born in heaven.

"At that time, bhikkhus, I was the teacher and these bhikkhus were the brahmin youths. Thus in the past as well I humbled these men when they were going about with their heads swollen with conceit."

Hearing this story of the past, thinking "In the past as well we were knocked down because of conceit," those bhikkhus became even more humble and applied themselves even more to their individual meditation subjects.

On a later occasion the Exalted One, walking on tour through the country, reached Vesālī, where he dwelt at the Gotamaka shrine. Knowing that the understanding of those five hundred bhikkhus had become mature, he taught them the Gotamaka Sutta (AN 3:123/A I 276): "Through direct knowledge *(abhiññāya),* bhikkhus, I teach Dhamma, not without direct knowledge. I teach a firmly grounded Dhamma with firm grounds *(sanidāna),* not groundlessly. I teach Dhamma that is convincing *(sappāṭihāriya),* not unconvincing. And since I teach Dhamma through direct knowledge, etc., my exhortation and my instruction should be put into practice. It is sufficient for you to

be pleased, bhikkhus, sufficient for you to be exultant, sufficient for you to be joyful: 'The Exalted One is a perfectly enlightened Buddha, the Dhamma is well-expounded, the Saṅgha is practising the good path.'" Thus spoke the Exalted One. And while this exposition was being spoken the ten thousandfold world system shook.

Having heard this sutta, those five hundred bhikkhus attained arahatship together with the four discriminations right in their very seats.[62] Thus on this occasion the present teaching (i.e., the Mūlapariyāya Sutta) reached the fulfilment of its purpose.

The Commentary to the Mūlapariyāya Sutta is concluded.

# NOTES

1. Because these defilements are the real causes for the "signs" (*nimitta*) the worldling perceives in things, they are called in the texts "sign-makers" (*nimittakaraṇa*): "Lust, friend, is a sign-maker, hatred is a sign-maker, delusion is a sign-maker" (MN 43.37/M I 298).

2. *Paṭhaviṃ maññati, paṭhaviyaṃ maññati, paṭhavito maññati, 'paṭhavī me' ti maññati.* In the translation below I have added parenthetical phrases to these statements for the sake of clarity; but in the light of the commentary even these will be seen to create an oversimplification of the meaning, and hence must be taken with reserve.

3. It cannot be stressed strongly enough, *contra* a number of popular expositions of the Buddhist point of view, that the ego-conception is not a product of social conditioning or of a misunderstanding of the abstractive character of language. The basic structure of the egoistic bias is already present *in toto* as a potential in the worldling's mental constitution from the moment of birth. It is an inherent concomitant of ignorance and craving, the causes of renewed birth. The impact of the environment calls forth the ego-notion in articulated form, but such an unfolding would not be possible if the basic disposition to egoistic distortion were not implicitly present from the start. In this connection see MN 64.3/M I 432, where the Buddha says that even in a little infant who does not have even an idea of a person, the latent tendency to personality view still lies dormant.

4. See MN 44.8/M I 300, etc.

5. Bhikkhu Ñāṇananda, *Concept and Reality in Early Buddhist Thought* (Kandy: Buddhist Publication Society, 1971), pp. 2–13.

6. Strictly speaking, all three notions, as deliberate considerations, are species of personality view. But insofar as the resulting views can be traced back to deeper psychological motives, the first and

second can be regarded as thematic justifications of craving and conceit.

7. See MN 72.15/M I 486; MN 109.13/M III 18, MN 112.11/M III 32, etc.

8. *Concept and Reality,* p.49.

9. Skt. Prajāpati, an ancient name for the supreme deity of early Indian religious thought. The commentary identifies him with Māra.

10. The reason for this peculiar conclusion is explained in the commentary. See also Introduction, pp. 21–22.

11. Various types of non-human beings. The *nāgas* are dragons, the *supaṇṇas* large birds, the *gandhabbas* celestial musicians, the *asuras* titans, and the *yakkhas* ogres.

12. The principal categories of Indian grammar.

13. "Personality" *(sakkāya)* here signifies the five clinging-aggregates *(pañcupādānakkhandhā)* which constitute the empirical being rather than character or personal temperament, as the word "personality" ordinarily suggests.

14. At the most basic ontological level the *dhamma* is identical with its *sabhāva* or specific nature. There is no real distinction between subject and predicate, between quality and bearer, and any such distinctions that occur in the exposition are mere concessions to ordinary usage for the purpose of communicating a particular point.

15. The "etc." may imply kamma and all other defilements.

16. This excludes all the dhammas of the supramundane plane—the four paths, fruits, and nibbāna.

17. Lit. "many person" or "herd person." The Pali word *puthu* actually represents two different Sanskrit words, *pṝthu,* many or numerous, and *pṝthak,* separate or distinct. Prefixed to the noun *jana,* "person," it gives the resultant compound a double significance: a common person, and a person who is distinct. The former is etymologically correct, but the latter also yields a pertinent meaning.

18. All etymological plays on the word "*ariyan.*"

19. These various types of insight knowledge are discussed in *Visuddhimagga,* Chapters 18–21. The Pali of this passage reads:

*Nāmarūpavavatthānena sakkāyadiṭṭhiyā; paccaya-pariggahena ahetuvisamahetudiṭṭhīnaṃ; tass'eva aparabhāgena kaṅkhāvitaraṇena kathaṃkathībhāvassa; kalāpasammasanena "ahaṃ mamā" ti gāhassa; maggāmaggavavatthānena amagge maggasaññāya; udayadassanena ucchedadiṭṭhiyā; vayadassanena sassatadiṭṭhiyā; bhayadassanena sabhaye abhayasaññāya; ādīnavadassanena assādasaññāya; nibbidānupassanāya abhiratisaññāya; muccitukamyatāñāṇena amuccitu-kamyatāya; upekkhāñāṇena anupekkhāya; anulomena dhammaṭṭhitiyaṃ nibbāne ca paṭilomabhāvassa; gotrabhunā saṅkhāranimittaggāhassa pahānaṃ; etaṃ tadaṅgapahānaṃ nāma.*

20. The word *dhamma* here is used in the sense of concrete actualities endowed with a specific nature. The individual *(puggala)* is a unified assemblage of such dhammas, not a concrete unity in its own right.

21. Vism 20.3–4; also commentary below.

22. According to the analysis of matter in the Abhidhamma, all matter contains at the minimum eight components—earth, water, fire, air, colour, smell, taste, and nutritive essence. Those species of matter in which the earth element is predominant are reckoned as "composite earth."

23. The *kasiṇa* is a circular disc exemplifying an element or a colour used as an object of concentration in the development of meditation.

24. This objection is framed by identifying the perception of characteristic earth with the penetration of the phenomenal characteristic through insight-wisdom. Since conceiving is incompatible with such penetration, the disputant tries to exclude characteristic earth from the bases of conceiving. But the subcommentator points out that the penetration of the characteristic through insight is not the meaning intended here.

25. The "etc." implies the other three perverted marks: permanent *(nicca),* pleasurable *(sukha)*, and self *(attā).*

26. Dhammas taking internal objects, dhammas taking external objects, and dhammas taking both internal and external objects. See Dhs §§1053–1055/Dhs 188.

27. The fact that this is a condensed interpretation implies that the conceivings can be extended to inanimate nature as well as to living beings.

28. The aggregate of material form, as including all types of matter, also includes the earth element, so when the former is mentioned the latter is implied.

29. According to the *Laws of Manu,* Mn 1.9, the seed deposited in the waters produced as the first creation of the Self-existent, became a golden egg, resplendent as the sun, in which the Self-existent Brahmā was born as Brahmā the Creator.

30. The "ancients" *(porāṇā)* are the early teachers whose interpretations of the canonical texts formed the basis for the old commentaries edited by Buddhaghosa.

31. These are the characteristics of craving, conceit, and views, respectively.

32. See Vism 20.18–19. Here, however, only forty modes are mentioned.

33. From the *Nettippakaraṇa,* a post-canonical exegetical treatise. Translated by Bhikkhu Ñāṇamoli as *The Guide* (London: Luzac & Co., 1962); see pp. 50–54 for treatment of this conveyance mode.

34. *Ye saṅkhāre upādāya sattā paññapīyanti.* This is said because "beings" are not individual concrete actualities existing in their own right, but assemblages of "formations" or conditioned mental and material dhammas conceptualized as unities with reference to these dhammas.

35. The lowest of the six sense sphere heavenly worlds.

36. The method for explaining perception is the same as that in the previous sections.

37. The administrative-warrior class of ancient Indian society.

38. The Buddhist holy day, observed on the new and full moon days.

39. *Mahā Aṭṭhakathā.* This is the primary source upon which Buddhaghosa based his own polished edition of the commentaries.

40. The highest of the six sense sphere heavenly worlds. The name means "wielding control over the creations of others."

41. For all these deities occupy a plane of existence determined by the kamma of the first jhāna attainment. In Buddhist cosmology the various planes of existence represent ontological counterparts of different states of consciousness, and are created by the kammic energy of the latter. A similar principle applies to the following classes of gods.

42. The wholesome in the case of non-arahat yogis who have attained to this base in meditation, the resultant in the case of beings reborn on this plane, and the inoperative in the case of arahats who have attained to this base in meditation.

43. According to the Pali commentaries, in contrast to seeing and hearing, the acts of smelling, tasting, and touching always involve direct contact of sense organ and object.

44. The word "trainee" might have been used, suggesting the practical nature of the learning-process undergone.

45. That is, the three ariyan individuals—a stream-enterer, once-returner, and non-returner.

46. The four bonds *(yoga)* are sensual desire, desire for existence, wrong views, and ignorance.

47. See above, pp. 49–50.

48. I have followed the second explanation of the subcommentary in the translation, which is the meaning the context seems to require, though the commentary gives a different explanation.

49. The Noble Eightfold Path in its supramundane aspect.

50. That is, they may become temporarily "devoid of lust" through the suppression of lust in the jhānas or meditative absorptions, but the latent tendency to lust *(rāgānusaya)* still remains ready to spring up again when conditions call it forth.

51. The commentary gives a detailed elaboration of each of these eight reasons, here omitted since it is included in my earlier work *Discourse on the All-Embracing Net of Views: The Brahmajāla Sutta and its Commentaries,* (Buddhist Publication Society, Kandy, 1978).

52. Vism 7.4–29.

53. For an explanation of these categories see Vism 17.287–297.

54. Of the four, delight = past active; suffering = present resultant; existence = present active; birth, ageing, and death = future resultant.

55. Present resultant existence involves the five beginning with consciousness; present active existence the five beginning with ignorance.

56. See Paṭis 1.275/Paṭis I 52.

57. The four paths of stream-entry *(sotāpatti),* once-returner *(sakadāgāmī),* non-returner *(anāgāmī),* and arahatship.

58. The famous Bodhi tree beneath which the Buddha attained enlightenment.

59. The four supramundane paths.

60. This is the stock canonical description of the learned brahmin.

61. J 245: *Kālo ghasati bhūtāni, sabbān'eva sah'attanā.*
*yo ca kālaghaso bhūto, sa bhūtapacaniṃ pacīti.*

62. The four discriminations *(paṭisambhidā)* are four types of specialized knowledge. They are the discrimination of meaning (or effect, *attha*); the discrimination of doctrine (or cause, *dhamma*); the discrimination of language (*nirutti*); and the discrimination of perspicuity (*paṭibhāna*), that is, the ability to utilize the former three kinds of knowledge in expounding the teaching. See Vism 14.21–31.

*Of related interest from the BPS*

## The All Embracing Net of Views

The Brahmajāla Sutta and its Commentaries
*Translated by Bhikkhu Bodhi*

The Brahmajāla, one of the Buddha's most important discourses, weaves a net of sixty-two cases capturing all the speculative views on the self and the world. The massive commentary and subcommentary allow for a close in-depth study of the work. The book contains a lengthy treatise on the Theravada conception of the Bodhisattva ideal. The long introduction is itself a modern philosophical commentary on the sutta.

BP 209S, 2006, 350 pp.

## Concept and Reality in Early Buddhist Thought

*Bhikkhu Ñāṇananda*

This is an important original work of Buddhist philosophy, dealing with the problem of what the author calls "conceptual proliferation" (*papañca*), the mind's tendency to distort reality through its own conceptual activity. Building upon a suggestive passage in the famous Madhupiṇḍika Sutta, the author develops a thesis which ties together many important but seldom explored strands in early Buddhist thought. The book contains profoundly illuminating remarks on obscure passages from the Pali Canon, and has significant implications for philosophy, psychology and ethics.

BP 404S, 1997, 170 pp.

*Of related interest from the BPS*

**The Life of the Buddha**
According to the Pāli Canon
*Bhikkhu Ñāṇamoli*

Numerous lives of the Buddha have been written and translated, but this volume, with its comprehensive material and original method of presentation, may well claim a place of its own. Composed entirely from texts of the Pāli Canon, the oldest authentic record, it portrays an image of the Buddha—the great Master of Wisdom and Compassion—which is vivid, warm, and moving. The ancient texts are rendered in a language marked by lucidity and dignity as befits the beauty of the original. They are presented in a framework of "narrators" and "voices" which serves to connect the canonical texts through historical notes and other informations thus giving coherence to the narrative. The book also includes a chapter on the Buddha's doctrine that is highly illuminating and has a distinct flavour of its own. This is a book that can inform and inspire.

BP 105S, 2006, 396 pp.

**The Great Discourse on Causation**
The Mahānidāna Sutta and Its Commentaries
*Translated by Bhikkhu Bodhi*

The Mahānidāna Sutta is the Buddha's longest discourse on dependent arising, often taken to be the key to his entire teaching. The commentary treats this doctrine according to the Abhidhamma method, explained in an appendix. A penetrative introduction lays bare the sutta's structure and the philosophical significance of dependent arising.

BP 211S, 2000, 160 pp.

## THE BUDDHIST PUBLICATION SOCIETY

The BPS is an approved charity dedicated to making known the Teaching of the Buddha, which has a vital message for all people.

Founded in 1958, the BPS has published a wide variety of books and booklets covering a great range of topics. Its publications include accurate annotated translations of the Buddha's discourses, standard reference works, as well as original contemporary expositions of Buddhist thought and practice. These works present Buddhism as it truly is—a dynamic force which has influenced receptive minds for the past 2500 years and is still as relevant today as it was when it first arose. For more information about the BPS and our publications, please visit our website or contact:


The Administrative Secretary
Buddhist Publication Society
P.O. Box 61
54 Sangharaja Mawatha
Kandy • Sri Lanka

Tel: 0094 81 223 7283 • Fax: 0094 81 222 3679
E-mail: bps@sltnet.lk
web site: http://www.bps.lk